(Front cover)
(top left) The **Mountwood***, with a capacity crowd aboard, heads down river from Seacombe on "Q.E.2 day", 24th July 1990. photo: Richard Danielson.*
(bottom left) Fondly remembered, the **Royal Iris** *in her green and yellow livery of the 1950s and 60s. The* **Wallasey Belle** *(see pages 40/41) once had a similar livery.*
(bottom right) The traditional waterfront view of Liverpool. The **Woodchurch** *is seen crossing the river on 9th February 1984. photo: Richard Danielson.*

(Inside front cover)
January 1963 found the River Mersey in the grip of very severe weather. photo: John Shepherd.

(Inside back cover)
Location chart of the River Mersey.

(Back cover)
The new livery chosen for the Mersey ferries after their major rebuilding in 1990 was very similar to the old colours of the Birkenhead Corporation ferries. The **Mountwood***, dressed overall, is seen here on 24th July 1990, sailing up river from Seacombe towards Birkenhead. In the background the three chimneys, locally called "the ugly sisters", are part of the now defunct Clarence Power Station, built on the site of the Clarence Dock, which closed to shipping after the great depression. photo: Richard Danielson.*

The Mighty
MERSEY
and its
FERRIES

by Richard Danielson

© Richard Danielson 1992
ISBN 0 9513155 4 4

FERRY Publications

D1340176

...s, Isle of Man, at P.O. Box 1, Laxey, Isle of Man
...work and Bureau Processing by Words & Spaces. Tel. 0624 662573
Text origination by The DeskTop Publishing Service, Douglas
Printed by Eyre & Spottiswoode Ltd., London and Margate

Contents

Foreword

The Mersey Ferries have played a major part in my life. For 25 years until my retirement as Editor of Sea Breezes magazine, I crossed the river between Birkenhead (Woodside) and Liverpool twice daily, sometimes more frequently. During that time I made many friends among the captains, mates and engineers on board and at a conservative estimate, I have made some 12,000 crossings.

Apart from "Ferries Forever", published a few years ago I know of no other book solely devoted to the Mersey ferries. That is why I welcome this book by my friend Richard Danielson, since it meets a particular need in the sphere of maritime literature.

In a book of this size, it has not been possible to deal in detail with the entire history of the ferries so the author has wisely concentrated on the years within living memory while touching on the origins of the service. In doing so he has produced a fascinating record of what are known as "The Famous Mersey Ferries".

Despite their fame, all has not been smooth sailing for the ferries. Threat of closure hung over them for a number of years as passenger numbers declined and losses mounted. Happily the Merseyside Passenger Transport Authority realised that a ferry presence on the river must be retained and took steps to ensure this.

As a result we still have ferries on the Mersey and although the changes made do not please everyone, they are far better than having no ferries at all.

I am sure this book will introduce the Mersey Ferries to a still wider public and I wish it every success.

Craig J. M. Carter
Higher Bebington

*The coal fired, steam powered Birkenhead ferry **Claughton** looks very stately in the late afternoon sun, as she approaches Woodside landing stage. The stern of one of the **Saxonia** class Cunarders can be seen alongside the Liverpool landing stage on the other side of the river. photo: Ray Pugh.*

Some personal reflections _____

Less than a decade after the end of World War 2, as a boy of about eight years old, I started spending many holidays on Merseyside. These were always spent with my father (himself an exiled Liverpudlian former seafarer), my grandparents who lived on the banks of the Manchester ship canal and my brother Martin.

Later, Martin had a very successful career in the merchant navy and became a deep sea Chief Engineer with Cayzer Irvine & Co. Limited's Clan Line Steamers before coming ashore for a top job in insurance.

Perhaps surprisingly, my own career path kept me on dry land and gradually led me into the board rooms of merchant banking where I now happily direct two banks, with the ferries still an all-engaging lifetime hobby.

Even as a young lad in the 1950s, I recognised the River Mersey as flowing with the lifeblood of that great "Scouse" metropolis, full as it then was with ocean liners, freighters, tankers bound for the oil termini, Isle of Man and Irish boats, pleasure steamers from North Wales and the ubiquitous Mersey ferries.

Winter and summer in all weathers, we spent hours going back and forth across the river and it was there, during those happy, formative years, that my love for the famous Mersey ferries was spawned. The first visit that I can recall clearly was in 1954 when I was nearly 8 years of age. The tragedy of the **Empress of Canada**, then recently salvaged (but totally devastated) dominated my perception of the Gladstone Dock where her burnt-out hulk lay as grim evidence of the spectre of fire aboard ship. A generation later, we live in the Isle of Man, so Liverpool remains our principal point of contact with the outside world for travel, major shopping or just a welcome change of scenery.

In addition to staying in Liverpool (where I first learnt to love the aroma of coffee beans freshly roasting in Coopers' Emporium and eating in J. Lyons' in Cook Street), many of those holidays were spent across the river at New Brighton. There, under the kindly eye of proprietress Mrs. Overs, for a few shillings per night bed and breakfast, we were welcomed year after year to her homely guest house above a gift and jewellery shop at number 74, Victoria Road. To see the summer show or pantomime at the Floral Pavilion was a staple part of our young lives.

In the evening, it was possible to see the Isle of Man Steamer and the North Wales boat coming up the Mersey together, the latter often having taken the now silted-up Rock Channel route, close to the New Brighton foreshore. As well as the New Brighton ferries, here too could be viewed the green and yellow painted, futuristic looking ferry **Royal Iris**, on her "fish and chip" cruises to the Bar Lightship (14 miles out to sea from Liverpool Pier Head).

Walking along the river inland from New Brighton, it was a healthy three mile stroll past the fair ground where once, long ago, stood a tower like the more famous one at Blackpool, an elevated tree walk (which was illuminated at night) and on along the promenade to Wallasey and the Seacombe ferry stage. Passing the Mariners' Rest Home and Egremont on the way, a stone promontory was all that remained as evidence of the earlier ferry service that once thrived there too.

At night, a glance across the river towards Liverpool revealed row upon row of ships in dock or anchored in the river awaiting orders (usually their funnels were floodlit). The occasional blast on a ship's whistle would abruptly shatter the otherwise perfect silence until the echo faded away far into the distance. The Irish boats traditionally sailed at night, as did extra Steam Packet ships engaged in the busy summer holiday trade bound for the Isle of Man. Tugs, coasters, pilot boats and other craft worked all round the clock and so too did the ferries, the subject of the book.

The harmonious chiming of the great illuminated clocks on the Royal Liver Building was a wonderful sound and means as much to lovers of Merseyside as does Big Ben to Londoners. The rattle of the chains on the ferry gangways being pulled up like drawbridges and a quick "toot" from the ferry whistle on its smoking funnel, combined to tell the world that the busy little ship was ready, even anxious, to get away. The ferry captain at his wheelhouse window ensured that all was well before calling for the necessary burst of effort to get his ship on the move.

A real treat was to be able to stay up late on New Year's Eve when, at the stroke of midnight, the whole river would come alive to the sound of ships' sirens and whistles welcoming in the New Year.

Going from Wallasey to Birkenhead Landing Stage on foot entailed walking through the Wallasey and Birkenhead dock systems as there was no promenade at this point on the river. Nominally guarded by a police constable in a red brick pill box, it was never actually difficult to obtain entry. Its dock workers and seamen, some noisy with the effects of ale (others just noisy), cobbled roadways with stray weeds and grasses forcing their way through the uneven granite sets, dockside railways and shunting steam engines, bollards and mooring ropes straining upwards, were all sights and sounds to complete the picture.

In winter, here one would find plenty of ferries laid up, gunwale to gunwale, with funnels and masts reaching skywards in sylvan fashion, awaiting their turn for seasonal service, overhaul or dry-docking. Slumbering Isle of Man boats could easily number seven or more and all these ships, together with the three vessels of the now much lamented Liverpool and North Wales Steamship Company filled the Morpeth, Morpeth Branch, Vittoria and other docks close by.

In those days, the ferries serving Birkenhead and Wallasey (plus New Brighton in the summer) were operated separately by the two local councils concerned. They both crossed the river from their respective landing stages and tied up at

*The cover of the interesting journal "Crossley Chronicles" shows the **Leasowe** arriving at New Brighton. The fog warning bell and its infamous lanyard (see page 8) can be clearly seen. Crossley Bros. Limited built diesel engines for the ferries.*

*Ferry trips up the Manchester ship canal have been popular for many decades. Here we see the **Egremont** negotiating Trafford Road Bridge (returning from Manchester) with plenty of school children aboard, including a party from Brandwood Street School.*
photo: Capt. Dennis Titherington collection.

Liverpool where the inland berths were used by the red funnelled Birkenhead boats and those nearer the sea by the then white funnelled ferries of the County Borough of Wallasey.

Liverpool's giant floating landing stage was half a mile long and designed to rise and fall with each tide. At peak times in summer, ferries from Birkenhead, Wallasey and New Brighton could be alongside, each loading at least a thousand passengers with other ferries waiting for a berth. Next could be the North Wales steamer with two thousand passengers aboard for a day trip to Llandudno, whilst immediately adjacent would be one or two well laden Steam Packet boats waiting to visit or returning from Mona's Isle, four hours steaming time away. Further along the landing stage downstream, Atlantic liners bound for Canada, North and South America and slightly smaller ships sailing to Mediterranean ports, Africa, the Middle and Far East would all embark their passengers there too. At the height of activity on the landing stage, the ferry captains would bring their busy little craft alongside with consummate skill, squeezing into berths seemingly no longer than the ferries themselves. Minutes later with a fresh load of passengers safely on board, they would leave again, springing off on a rather frayed looking rope, invariably against the tide.

There was always a tremendous "air of expectancy" down on the landing stage!

The famous Liverpool Overhead Railway served the whole six and a half miles of the dock system which ran from Dingle to Seaforth and earned the elevated electric train system the nickname, "The Dockers' Umbrella". Today, Seaforth is renowned for its massive container terminal which continues to exceed cargo handling records and is the success story of the decade. The Overhead Railway (the last remains of which it is still possible to find along its old route) opened in 1893 and its demise came as late as 1956 by which time more and more people were travelling to Liverpool by car or electric train. It was never part of British Railways and remained independent until the end. Before the opening of the tunnels under the Mersey, the majority of Liverpool's non-resident workforce came to work by ferry from across the river, and thousands daily then took the Overhead Railway to their place of work. Those who did not travel the "Overhead" joined the trams that, until not so very long ago, marshalled at the Pier Head.

In the days that the ferries were the main means for workers to cross the river, it was recognised that the later the ferry one took to work in the morning, the more senior was one's position. By the time that the 9 o'clock boat was able to be caught, one really was someone!

Liverpool's Pier Head waterfront is world renowned, dominated by the Royal Liver Building which bears the legendary Liver bird at the top of each of its two main towers. Half cormorant, half eagle, with a piece of seaweed in its beak, the great bird symbolises Liverpool's almost eight hundred year connection with commerce and the sea.

The Liverpool Landing Stage that was in use in the 1950s (since replaced with a modern one) consisted mainly of wooden sections on huge metal flotation tanks. It was secured to the land by hinged wrought iron and steel covered bridges and a sectioned, floating roadway (the latter originally constructed for the horse-drawn vehicles using the old "luggage boats"), all of which enabled it to float up and down with the tide. Busking musicians and actors, flower sellers and others, were also to be seen going about their business within the relative shelter of the landing stage approaches. On its massive wooden deck, iron pillars and wrought iron arches rose gracefully upwards carrying a metal roof of some architectural beauty. There was a bookstall and also a café / tea room with steamed up windows, where one could wait for the ferries.

During winter, the scene could be less than inviting. In gales that so often blow up and down the Mersey, the whole landing stage would heave up and down just like a ship at sea, but with the added trauma of its sectioned length snakily following the contours of the waves beneath. High winds, laden with salt spray, rain or snow, could make it a very hostile place to stand and wait for a ferry (or to spend one's working day if one worked for the ferries) but people travelled in their thousands. It seemed even worse after dark with the elements so much more accentuated. Sometimes in bad weather the boats, particularly the old steam ferries, struggled and strained to get off the stage only to come crashing back alongside as wave after wave pounded at their exposed beam. For passengers it was always as well to be ready for such excitement. For the unwary, the experience usually resulted in being thrown off balance just at the crucial moment when ship and landing stage made unexpected contact again and the rubber tyre between them screamed in protest, whilst any shape it might once have had, was squeezed from it! Under these extreme conditions, mooring ropes securing a ferry to the stage would stretch and groan to the point that breaking seemed inevitable - but they almost never did.

Fog too was a nightmare for the ferry captains and before radar came in 1949, they had to grope their way across the river, listening out both for any sound of impending collision and also for the clanging bell on the distant landing stage which provided an audible target for which to aim! Birkenhead, Wallasey and Liverpool all had mechanically operated fog bells but the one at New Brighton remained manually operated. It had a long lanyard running from the bell to the sleeping bunk of the stageman whose duty was to ring the bell every minute throughout the day and night during fog! Despite all this, the ferries kept sailing, providing that all-important connection and for the thousands of people who sailed every day of every week, life without them would have been unthinkable.

The incomparable **Royal Iris** *heads up river towards Liverpool's famous Pier Head.*   photo: Capt. Dennis Titherington collection.

In the beginning

If ferries can be said to have "roots" then those of the ferries across the Mersey go down a long way, through many centuries to the Middle Ages.

History shows that a Benedictine Priory was founded on the Wirral in or about the year 1150 and some time thereafter its monks began a ferry service for their own benefit. This marked the beginning of the Birkenhead ferry as we know it today. In those days, the fare on market day was recorded as being "one penny for a man and what he could carry". In the year 1207, Liverpool (then no more than an unknown, minor village) was created "A Free Borough on the Sea" by letters patent of King John. Early references describe the ferry as the "King's bote in Mersee".

On 13th April 1330, King Edward III confirmed to the Prior and Convent of Birkenhead, the licence to operate a ferry across the Mersey and to do other relevant things. His Majesty stated his willingness to:

do still more abundant favour both to the traveller and the monks.

Translated from the original Latin of the Royal decree, its immortal authority said the following:

That they and their successors for ever might have the passage over the said arm of the sea, as well as for man as for horses as for other things whatsoever and may receive for the passage what is reasonable without let or hindrance.

It was an extension of his father's licence of 1317 wherein the Prior of Birkenhead (then Byrkehaved, Byrkhed or Byrkheved) gained specific (but not wholly satisfactory), rights:

To erect lodging houses and buy and sell provisions for the support of the men thereabout to cross the said arm of the sea

and,

on account of great contriety of weather and frequent storms.

Created by the King of England, it would take an Act of Parliament to change the protected status of the Birkenhead ferry and despite the events of 1977 (of which we shall read

more later) the same is still true to this day.

Throughout Britain, and in this the Mersey ferries were no exception, ancient ferry rights and charters ranked high amongst gifts and privileges that could be bestowed by the monarchy. The Burgesses of Liverpool were exempt from ferry tolls. By then Liverpool had started to grow in stature and its importance was gaining national recognition. King Henry VIII is recorded as accusing Liverpool of defrauding the monarchy and in 1528 appointed a commission to look into:

all royal fish, wrecks, flotsam, jetsam etc. coming falling or happening in the stream and water called Mersey.

Consequent upon the Dissolution of the Monasteries in 1536, the Priory at Birkenhead was seized by the Crown and sold in 1545 and the ferry is noted passing to Sir Ralph Worsley.

Early records of what is now the Wallasey ferry further downstream, describe the "Passage of Seccum" and the operation of the ferry from a stone slipway at Seacombe. However, the very earliest ferries at Seacombe are believed to have sailed across Wallasey Pool on the same side of the river, necessitating the crossing of the river to take place via the Birkenhead Priors' ferry. Later, Seacombe was provided with a drawbridge type arrangement to allow access at various states of the tide to save the inconvenience of having to wade ashore. On the other side of the river at Liverpool a berth, near where St. Nicholas' Church now stands with a slipway extending to the low water mark, was provided.

It took many years for ownership of the ferries and the various ferry rights to be settled and in the three centuries from 1545, Birkenhead and the other up river ferries changed hands countless times resulting in many leases being granted for their operation. In the end, as we shall see in the next chapter, the important commercial ones came under Local Government control, whilst others (seemingly less vital) gradually faded into obscurity. The Wallasey area ferries were no different and went through many changes of ownership too. The changes often resulted in or from complicated transactions involving not just the ferries (but land, hotels, piers, jetties, railways) whilst other changes were by inheritance.

Sadly, space does not permit us to explore all the old and minor, separate ferries of which there were many, nor those which did not eventually come under local government control.

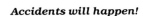

Accidents will happen!

(above) The **Leasowe** *was unlucky enough to be in collision with the* **Royal Daffodil II** *on 7th April 1960 and again with the Belfast Steamship Company's ferry* **Ulster Prince** *on 19th April 1960. One consolation was that both damaged her in exactly the same place! The* **Leasowe** *went into Cammell Laird's ship repair yard on 16th May 1960 for all the damage to be made good.* photo: Malcolm McRonald.

(right) *On 19th September 1991 the* **Mountwood** *briefly ran out of control and hit the landing stage at Liverpool causing £30,000 worth of damage to her bow.*
photo: Mersey Ferries.

10

Sail gives way to steam

The "ancestral" ferries, which were small sailing vessels and rowed craft (manned by burly, often none too pleasant boatmen) gave way to the first purpose built, regular steam powered ferries in 1822, whilst just prior to this, various steamers had operated on a trial basis only. On the Woodside service there was introduced a wooden paddle steamer named **Royal Mail** whilst at Seacombe, a ship aptly named **Seacombe** started at about the same time. The earliest powered ferries also doubled as tugs much to the consternation of would-be ferry passengers, who often found that their return trip had been delayed by hours as the ferry had gone off on a lucrative tow! The operations of the up river "Birkenhead" ferry routes and the down river "Wallasey" ferries were distinct and quite unconnected. They remained so, gradually rationalising and merging until the marriage of the two Corporations' fleets was finally completed, about a century and a half later.

From the mid-1800s the railways became involved in ownership of, or had operational agreements with, some of the ferry routes and, like the ferries themselves, it should be remembered that Britain's railways were also all separately owned and operated. Almost universally, the railways came before the trunk roads yet merchants' horse-drawn carts, carriages and stage coaches etc. made up a large part of the ferry traffic of the period. It was not until 1886 that the first railway tunnel under the Mersey was opened and with it came the most serious challenge to the ferries' supremacy. Originally steam hauled, in 1903 the line was electrified. Before this, it had been conceived that the ferries might carry railway wagons across the river using a specially constructed terminal at Seacombe, but the plan did not materialise for want of suitable facilities at the Liverpool side.

The important up river ferries were the first to come under local government control, passing to Birkenhead local commissioners in a lengthy transaction set up under the Birkenhead Improvement Acts in 1842 but not completed for sixteen years. The Eastham Ferry remained in private hands connected to the pleasure gardens and hotel until 1929 when the commercial battle was finally lost and the ferry ceased. Twenty years after that process started, the Wallasey ferry became vested in the Wallasey Local Government Board in 1862. In the case of Birkenhead, the several different up river ferries were still separate prior to coming under community control. By way of contrast, in the twenty years that separated that happening at Wallasey, the three Wallasey area ferries (Seacombe, Egremont and New Brighton) had already come under the common control of the Coulborn family, so needed no further amalgamation.

In addition to the present service to Woodside (Birkenhead) and Seacombe (Wallasey), over the years, ferry services have operated from Liverpool to:- New Brighton (until 1971), Egremont (until 1941), old Birkenhead (until 1872), Monks Ferry (until 1878), Tranmere (until 1904), Rock Ferry (until 1939), New Ferry (until 1924), Eastham (until 1929), Ellesmere Port and Runcorn (until mid 1850s), and the Otterspool Flower Festival site during 1984/85.

Unlike Liverpool and the populated areas of the Wirral on the other side of the river which had evolved through natural population growth, New Brighton and Eastham were "created". New Brighton owes its existence to Everton builder James Atherton who, in 1830 bought 170 acres of land (mainly wind-blown sand dunes) on the extreme seaward side of the Wirral peninsular upon which to construct "a fashionable watering place". His vision was for "every house to have an uninterrupted view of the sea". Its ferry started in 1833 and ran to Liverpool from where much of the New Brighton affluence emanated. It gained great popularity, particularly in Edwardian times, as a resort which was something of an up-market Blackpool. The Tower Building at New Brighton, complete with its tower stood 621 feet high and was, at one time, the country's tallest man-made edifice.

The Eastham ferry will best be remembered for its three main ferries named **Pearl**, **Ruby** and **Sapphire** built by J. Jones, Liverpool in 1897/98 and which (except for admiralty war service) remained faithful to the Eastham ferry until its end in 1929.

The choice of names for the Corporation ferries is interesting and was, for many years, individual to the two local councils which operated them.

The principal vessels of what became the Birkenhead Corporation fleet were generally named after real places, mostly areas of the Wirral or Lancashire.

Since 1863 their ships have been named thus:-

Cheshire (paddle/1863/421 gross tons),

Lancashire (paddle/1865/389 gross tons),

Woodside (paddle/1865/373 gross tons, sold to Wallasey fleet in 1891 for use as a vehicle ferry),

Claughton (paddle/1876/596 gross tons),

Oxton (vehicle ferry, twin screw sets fore and aft/1879/431 gross tons), renamed **Old Oxton** 1925,

Bebington (vehicle ferry, twin screw sets fore and aft/1880/435 gross tons), renamed **Old Bebington** 1925,

Birkenhead (paddle/bought 1880/ 448 gross tons),

Tranmere (vehicle ferry, twin screw fore and aft/1884/435 gross tons),

Cheshire (paddle/1889/380 gross tons),

Mersey (twin screw/1890/391 gross tons),

Wirral (twin screw/1890/391 gross tons),

Birkenhead (paddle/1894/434 gross tons),

Lancashire (twin screw/1899/469 gross tons),

Claughton (twin screw/1899/469 gross tons), renamed **Old Claughton** 1930,

Bidston (twin screw/1903/444 gross tons), renamed **Old Bidston** 1933,

Woodside (twin screw/1903/444 gross tons),

Prenton (vehicle ferry, twin screw sets fore and aft/1906/487 gross tons),

Storeton (twin screw/1910/342 gross tons),

Barnston (vehicle ferry, twin screw sets fore and aft/1921/724 gross tons),

Churton (vehicle ferry, twin screw sets fore and aft/1921/724 gross tons).

The remainder of the Birkenhead fleet to date is detailed later within the text.

Whilst the Birkenhead fleet had its formal geographic naming process, its counterparts at Wallasey adopted flower names as their principal theme. However, theirs was not an exclusive nomenclature as it also included place names in the area and those of former Chairmen of the Council Ferry Committee.

Since 1862, the Wallasey Corporation controlled fleet of ferries has been named thus:-

Water Lily (paddle/1862/204 gross tons),

May Flower (paddle/1862/241 gross tons),

Wild Rose (paddle/1862/132 gross tons),

Heather Bell (paddle/1863/205 gross tons),

Maggie (single screw, small coaling barge),

Swallow (paddle/bought 1872/93 gross tons),

Seymour (paddle/bought 1872/110 gross tons),

Sunflower (built for but unsuccessful carrying vehicles/paddle/1879/345 later 242 when rebuilt),

Daisy (paddle/1879/285 gross tons),

Primrose (paddle/1880/285 gross tons),

Wallasey (vehicle ferry, twin screw sets fore and aft/1881/459 gross tons),

Violet (paddle/1883/273 gross tons),

Crocus (twin screw sets fore and aft but not a vehicle ferry/1884/301 gross tons),

Snowdrop (twin screw sets fore and aft but not a vehicle ferry/ 1884/300 gross tons),

Thistle (paddle/1891/301 gross tons),

Shamrock (on acquisition became a vehicle ferry/paddle/ bought from Birkenhead 1891/377 gross tons),

Emily (single screw coaling barge/1895/154 gross tons),

John Herron (paddle/1896/333 gross tons),

Pansy (paddle/1896/333 gross tons),

Tulip (dredger for use at New Brighton/1898/409 gross tons),

Rose (twin screw/1900/514 gross tons),

Lily (twin screw/1901/514 gross tons),

Seacombe (vehicle ferry, twin screw sets fore and aft/ 1901/589 gross tons),

Iris, later renamed ***Royal Iris*** (twin screw/1906/465 gross tons),

Daffodil, later renamed ***Royal Daffodil*** (twin screw/ 1906/465 gross tons),

Bluebell, later renamed ***John Joyce*** (twin screw/1910/ 439 gross tons),

Snowdrop (twin screw/1910/439 gross tons),

Emily II (another small coaling barge bought 1933).

The remaining units of the Wallasey ferry fleet to date are dealt with later in the text.

> Old ferry publicity material depicting a venerable Wallasey Corporation ferry captain on the bridge of his ship, appears in the records and has a title worthy of mention:- "Your safety and comfort is in the hands of experienced men".

(top right) The **Egremont** *on winter service. The awnings above her top deck were constructed of wood whereas those on her sister, the* **Leasowe***, were canvas. photo: Capt. Dennis Titherington collection.*

(bottom right) The **Marlowe** *"rounding to" at Seacombe in a force 10 storm. In other literature this photograph has been described as showing the* **Royal Iris.** *photo: Mersey Ferries archives.*

The **Blarney**, (see page 17) *was none other than the 1906* **Royal Iris** *photo: Alex Duncan, Gravesend.*

The **Shandon**, (see page 35) *was previously the* **John Joyce.** *photo: Alex Duncan, Gravesend.*

Sold for further service

The **Betula** (see page 38) *was previously the last of the Wallasey "luggage boats" and was named* **Perch Rock.** *photo: John Collins.*

The **Haringvliet** (see page 40) *is virtually unrecognisable as the former* **Royal Iris** *of 1932. She is seen here arriving at Middelharnis on 12th June 1959. photo: Craig J.M. Carter.*

First World War epic

During the First World War many great feats of courage and bravery were recorded. One particular event of immense merit, involving two Mersey ferries, took place during the famous Zeebrugge (and Ostend) Raids.

Under plans, the necessity for which was perceived in 1917 under Sir John Jellicoe (before his resignation as First Sea Lord) but later amended by his successor, Wemyss and Vice Admiral Sir R. Keyes R.N., a way had been devised to curtail the comings and goings of the German U-boat fleet based at Bruges. The U-boats had exits to the sea via Zeebrugge and Ostend canals and under the scheme, blockships were to be sunk in the entrances to both, in a way crucial to achieving the U-boats' long term immobilisation.

After two earlier abortive attempts, the night finally chosen was 22nd/23rd April 1918, having the best combination of darkness, high water at the right time, a calm sea and some onshore wind, the latter to fan the proposed smokescreen. The attack was to be on St. George's Day and late on the 22nd, the special convoy set sail from a creek in the Thames Estuary. The raiding party and its support, included H.M.S. **Vindictive** dating from 1897, the destroyer H.M.S. **Warwick** and others, the blockships themselves, C Class submarines laden with explosives, ships from the Dover Patrol and two humble Mersey ferries taken from their normal duties for this vital mission. Wing Commander F.A. Brock R.N.A.S., a director of the famous manufacturer of fireworks had devised a smoke screen which needed no visible flame as its source. He took part in the raid but sadly, died on the mole at Zeebrugge but not before he had seen his invention at work. The smoke, which was duly laid by some sixty two naval motor launches (M.Ls.) provided vital cover until just before midnight, but unfortunately, the wind changed direction at the worst possible time, again leaving the main raiding party openly exposed to the German onslaught from the land.

Nevertheless, for the old light cruiser H.M.S. **Vindictive** (equipped with flame-throwers and mortars) together with the troop-carrying Mersey ferries **Iris** and **Daffodil** (both 1906/465 gross tons) there was no turning back. The ferries were selected for their light draught and because their hull framing extended to the upper deck. Requisitioned on 12th February 1918, they had received special bullet proof plating to help protect their otherwise open upperworks. The troops aboard the **Iris** and the **Daffodil** were to overcome the German defences on the mole thus allowing the planned sinking of the concrete laden blockships to take place, supposedly prohibiting the U-boats' exits. Their job included having to land a storming party and take the 5.9 inch gun battery that guarded the entrance to the harbour.

Finally, without the protection of the smokescreen which the wind was dispersing in the wrong direction, the main raid

The legendary **Royal Iris** *and* **Royal Daffodil** *seen here at Liverpool after their Zeebrugge exploits had left them famous, but well and truly battle scarred.* photo: Merseyside Record Office.

was a bloody affair. At 00.01, H.M.S. **Vindictive** went in, bravely accompanied by the Mersey ferries, **Daffodil** and **Iris**. The ferries were attacked time and again and it speaks volumes for their robust constitutions that they survived their ordeal. They gave everything they had and the **Daffodil** came alongside H.M.S. **Vindictive** and helped by pressing her against the mole, there being no other way of mooring or berthing the vessel under such intense enemy fire.

Over an hour later, when they had completed their duties the turn came for the **Iris** to leave Zeebrugge. Reports show that almost defenceless and very vulnerable, she was receiving terrible punishment from enemy shore-based units. Sensing the **Iris's** desperate plight, the naval launch **M.L. 558** (carrying the commander of the whole M.L. flotilla) put herself between the much slower ferry and the mole, laying down a smokescreen and drawing off enemy fire as she sped past.

The **Iris's** situation was perilous but, urged on by her engineers, her faithful steam engines responded with every ounce of power they could deliver and under the protective mantle of the life-giving smokescreen, the **Iris** made good her escape.

The **Daffodil** received heavy shell damage to her hull which penetrated the plating and caused major flooding of some of the compartments. Both ships were severely strafed by artillery and machine gun fire and the **Iris** had the port side of her bridge and her starboard forward gangway door completely shot away.

The **Iris** and the **Daffodil**, together with H.M.S. **Vindictive** and the other naval ships which they had so ably supported during the raid, returned to Dover in severely damaged condition, with the **Daffodil** gratefully accepting a tow from the destroyer H.M.S. **Trident**.

A few days later on 10th May H.M.S. **Vindictive** returned to Ostend where she was deliberately sunk at the lock gates.

214 people were killed and 383 were wounded in the raids and their supreme sacrifice is to this day still remembered in a commemoration service held at sea every year, aboard one of the Mersey ferries. Years ago, the records show that these services of remembrance were held in the vestibule at Seacombe booking hall.

In recognition of the conspicuous and valiant parts played by the **Iris** and the **Daffodil**, the Admiralty Secretary, on behalf of the Lords' Commissioners of the Admiralty, wrote to Wallasey Corporation thus:

*My Lords venture to express their confidence that the gallant exploit at Zeebrugge on April 23, in which the **Iris** and **Daffodil** took such a prominent part has been appreciated by the Wallasey Council and the public who journey by these ferry steamers more intimately from their local connection with these vessels. The services of the **Iris** and **Daffodil** were invaluable for the success of the operation.*

Also, immediately after the action, on 24th April Vice Admiral Sir R. Keyes R.N. wired to the ferries manager:

I am sure it will interest you to know that your two stout vessels carried Royal Navy sailors (Bluejackets) and Marines to Zeebrugge and remained alongside the mole for an hour, greatly contributing to the success of the operation. They will return to you directly the damage caused by the enemy gun fire has been repaired.

With these and numerous other testimonials to hand, at their meeting held on 2nd May 1918, Wallasey County Borough Council resolved to petition His Majesty King George V for permission to add "Royal" to the names of the two gallant ferries. The text of that Petition is as opposite.

At the subsequent council meeting on 30th May 1918, the following was noted:

*The Town Clerk submitted a letter from the Home Office intimating that the Council's Petition as to the **Iris** and the **Daffodil** had been placed before the King, and that His Majesty had been*

TO THE KINGS MOST EXCELLENT MAJESTY.

The Humble Petition of the Corporation of the County Borough of Wallasey, in the County of Cheshire.

MOST GRACIOUS SOVEREIGN

We the Mayor, Alderman and Burgesses of the County Borough of Wallasey humbly pray that Your Majesty may deign to sanction the use of the names **Royal Daffodil** *and* **Royal Iris** *for the two Ferry Steamers* **Daffodil** *and* **Iris** *which, after being taken over by Your Majesty's Navy, took part in the recent memorable attack upon Zeebrugge. These Ferry Steamers are the property of your Petitioners. The great number of passengers per annum carried between the County Borough and the City of Liverpool, twenty-nine millions per annum, naturally arouses a greater amount of interest than usual in these two ferry boats, and Your Majesty's gracious sanction to the prayer of this Petition will give great satisfaction not only to the inhabitants of the County Borough but also to a large number of visitors who use the ferry steamers. It may perhaps be within the recollection of Your Majesty that when you laid the foundation stone of the new Town Hall, Wallasey, Her Most Gracious Majesty The Queen and Yourself crossed the Mersey on the S.S.* **Daffodil.**

Your Petitioners humbly pray that Your Majesty will be pleased to accede to their request.

And your Petitioners will ever pray etc.,

The Common Corporate Seal of the Mayor, Aldermen and Burgesses of the County Borough of Wallasey was hereunto affixed this 2nd day of May 1918 in the presence of:

Frank F Scott, Mayor.

H W Cook, Town Clerk.

"*graciously pleased to accede to the prayer thereof*" *and to command that the ferry steamships* **Daffodil** *and* **Iris** *which took part in the attack on Zeebrugge, should be renamed* **Royal Daffodil** *and* **Royal Iris.**

Tired and battle scarred but with pennants proudly flying, the two ships returned home to the Mersey and whilst still in naval grey, complete with gunfire and explosion damage, they were placed on exhibition to the public in Liverpool.

A further minute dated 19th July 1918 in the Wallasey County Borough Council records, resolved that:

arrangements be made for the renaming ceremony and that Mrs. Farley, wife of the Council Chairman, be requested to officiate.

The renaming was to take place in dock followed by a river trip for wounded soldiers.

After major refits, they both returned to their ferry and cruising duties.

In 1923, the **Royal Iris** became the official cruise boat of the Wallasey fleet and was given a grey hull to go with her otherwise standard colour scheme. She was sold on 12th October 1931, (for the princely sum of £2,100) to Messrs. Palmer Bros. for further service in Dublin Bay. She was sold by them to Cork Harbour Commissioners in 1946 for yet more service in Irish waters. There she was appropriately named **Blarney** and kept her passenger certificate for 1,600 until she was scrapped in 1961 at the ripe old age of 55! The **Royal Daffodil** took over as cruise ship and was also given the special grey livery. She remained in the fleet until 30th October 1933, when she was sold for £2,515 to the General Steam Navigation company's associate, New Medway S.P. Company (owners of the famous paddle steamer, **Medway Queen**) for excursions from Rochester and Southend. In contrast to her sister's longevity, the **Royal Daffodil** lasted only until 1938 before being scrapped in Ghent.

*The Captain orders full power for the **Overchurch** as she battles with the elements on 28th October 1989 when severe gales swept the Mersey and the north west of England. She is seen here in the "Flower Festival" livery.*

photo: Richard Danielson.

18

*The **Overchurch** seen wearing the yellow/blue funnel livery of the Merseyside Passenger Transport Authority on 5th October 1974.*
photo Malcolm McRonald.

In addition to carrying tens of millions of foot passengers each year (and some with cycles, motorcycles and packages) on the ferry services and ever popular cruises, the carriage of vehicles across the river also became big business. It was always subject to tidal interference which, in the Mersey produces a rise and fall of up to 30 feet, twice every day. In the Birkenhead Guide of 1853 we read as follows:

In 1847, The Great Landing Stage was opened to the public. This is one of the lions of the river and deserves particular notice. The approaches are by two bridges, one North, one South. It is the largest and most extraordinary stage ever constructed - the length being 508 feet and the breadth 82 feet and the depth 9 feet 2 inches. It floats upon iron pontoons.

It was rebuilt on more massive proportions in 1874, but prior to its official opening, a fire started by a gas-fitter completely gutted the new stage which took another two years to rebuild. The landing stage eventually had three sections providing berthage for passenger ferries, vehicle ferries until 1947 (with its associated floating roadway) and North Wales and Isle of Man steamers, liners and other craft. In 1921 work commenced to enable it to be lengthened to accommodate an extra steamer. In that form, it served its intended purpose very well for another fifty years but by March 1973 it was well past its prime and demolition of the superstructure commenced. It was finally completely replaced by a shorter, modern floating concrete stage a century after its debut. The new stage is used by the ferries, Isle of Man boats, pilot launches and an assortment of tugs and other craft. For a long while the old floating roadway survived, still in use connected to the new stage, but by 1990, its demolition and removal was complete. As a major part of the grand refurbishment programme of 1990, the Liverpool ferry terminal and a new ticket office were created and adorned with an attractive structure resembling a marquee, which has a certain futuristic look about it. A warm and comfortable new waiting room was constructed on the landing stage at the same time.

Birkenhead constructed the first floating landing stage on the other side of the river in 1861/62, but it was not until six years later that the construction of its associated floating roadway was completed. The seaward end of the Woodside stage was used for landing cattle. The Birkenhead floating roadway was removed in 1958 and the whole structure was replaced during 1985/86 with a brightly painted single berth, modern stage, complete with new passenger bridges, approaches and renovated terminal (the latter being a listed building). New Brighton followed in 1867 and in 1880, Wallasey having by then become a popular residential commuter area, also had a new floating stage constructed. The Wallasey terminal was (and to this day remains) built on land reclaimed from the riverbank. Despite hinged bridges capable of taking foot passengers, prior to the floating roadways being constructed, bulky goods and larger vehicles for shipment had to be raised by hydraulic lifts from river level to the land. At low water, this process must have been as laborious as it was time consuming, and involved unhitching horses from horse-drawn carts etc. before loading could take place.

The ships themselves (not surprisingly as they had a well defined common purpose) evolved along the same naval architectural theme which reached something of a pinnacle in 1900 with the building of the Wallasey ferry, **Rose**. She is regarded as being the "mother" of all later ferries. Paddles gave way to propellers well over a century ago but it was not until late in 1949 with the arrival of the **Channel/Wallasey Belle**, followed by the **Royal Iris** and the **Leasowe** in 1951 that in the end, steam (raised first by burning coal and then by oil) was finally replaced by diesel. The ferries provided a good testing ground for new and innovative ship design skills and all embodied the latest thoughts on reliability, subdivision and passenger safety. The River Mersey was uncomfortably busy, often quite rough and regularly shrouded in fog.

The ships had to be good, tough specimens.

Some vehicles were carried on the old passenger ferries but in 1879, the Wallasey operation acquired three paddle steamers, one of which was named **Sunflower**. She was built for use as a vehicle carrier with large, overhanging decks to increase her payload but was unsuccessful thus. Suitably rebuilt, she made an excellent conventional passenger boat and lasted in service until 1905.

In 1879 the first purpose built vehicular ferry (collectively they became know as the "goods boats" or "luggage boats") came on the Birkenhead service. Devoid of any real superstructure, both the **Oxton** (431 gross tons) and, a year later, the **Bebington** (435 gross tons) had a large, open main vehicle deck on which were also borne the funnel, cowls, wheelhouse and ticket office. Their compound steam engines powered two sets of twin screws, fore and aft and as a class, they were very manoeuvrable. Their predecessors had all been paddle driven. They provided the basic design for their successors and those at Wallasey that followed, the first of which was aptly named **Wallasey** (459 gross tons) when built in 1881. Their appearance was indicative of the tasks they were intended to perform and whilst their looks may not have been their greatest asset, they certainly had a purposeful air about them.

By July 1925 a regular Sunday "luggage boat" service proved necessary. In February 1929 the records show that the Birkenhead Goods Service was being maintained via Seacombe ferry - five boats (3 Birkenhead, 2 Wallasey) during reconstruction of Woodside floating roadway.

The New Brighton landing stage was replaced by a new one in 1921. 1925/6 saw the Wallasey Stage replaced with a larger one capable of handling three ferries and, for the first time, with the benefit of a floating roadway in place of the old lifts system which had survived all those years! The new roadway was opened by the Earl of Derby on 23rd October

Liverpool landing stage in the 1960s.   photo: Ray Pugh.

The old Birkenhead booking hall. The landing stage was replaced in 1985/86 but the booking hall could only be refurbished, as it is a listed building.   photo: John Collins.

1926. The original Wallasey ferry buildings were demolished in 1932 and, in the ensuing two years, were rebuilt complete with a clock tower that remains a focal point on the river. Further major rebuilding work and the provision of new shore facilities was finished in 1991 including the provision of the so called Seacombe Sub-Marine - a bright new aquarium and restaurant facility. The New Brighton ferry called at Egremont on the way (in both directions) and operated all the year round until 1935, during which winter, the ferry terminated at Egremont. In 1936 and annually thereafter until its closure, it operated in the summer months only. The Egremont ferry, which had its own iron pier and floating stage finally ceased in 1941 after various ships had collided with the pier. New Brighton remained a popular tourist resort well into the 1960s, latterly with a cable chair lift running up to the top of the Tower Building. The tower itself was completed in 1900 but fell into disrepair

during the First World War and was demolished in 1920 after a relatively short lifespan. Sadly, the Tower Building then had a serious fire in April 1969 and it too, had to be demolished. There was also a fun fair, miniature railway, the world's largest swimming pool and marine boating lake to name but a few of many leisure amenities.

Under the auspices of the Merseyside Municipal Co-ordination Committee formed in 1922, plans were laid which culminated in the opening of the first road tunnel under the Mersey. This tunnel to Birkenhead (the first of two across the Mersey) was known as the Queensway Tunnel and was to be yet another major challenge to the ferries. In its own way, the road tunnel was more life-threatening than the advent of the railways on the Mersey scene. 1934 saw the tunnel (which was then the world's largest) completed at a time when the family car was yet to become really popular. The Birkenhead ferries received a cash subsidy from the new road tunnel in

The original Mersey road tunnel to Birkenhead was completed in 1934. Thirty seven years later, a second road tunnel was constructed, this time to Wallasey.   photo: George Danielson collection.

The **Wallasey** "rounding to" at New Brighton with good load of passengers aboard.   photo: Ray Pugh.

lieu of the business thereby lost.

Horse-drawn vehicles and certain lorries (many of which were still steam powered in those days), vehicles carrying oil, petroleum and other specified hazardous products were prohibited from using the tunnel and for a while, they therefore carried on the time honoured use of the "luggage boats". The tunnel cost £7,475,500 and involved the excavation of 1,200,000 tons of mainly sandstone rock. Persons involved in the building of the tunnel, tell fascinating stories of how the concrete used in its construction was forced up, under pressure through uncharted fissures in the rock, finding its way into the ground floors and basements of Birkenhead properties!

In 1971, a second tunnel, the Kingsway, was opened for traffic from Wallasey. These days in the 1990s both tunnels are very busy and a recent record was established when 500,000 vehicles per week drove through the two road tunnels under the Mersey. The present toll is 60p for a car which is insufficient to repay early losses and finance charges built up over the years and there is talk of a new £1.00 toll being introduced.

In 1937, a new Co-ordination Committee, which by then included Liverpool, Wallasey, Birkenhead, the Mersey Docks and Harbour Board and others on its board was set up. It considered all matters relating to cross river services, closure of the Rock Ferry service, continued use of the "luggage boats" and the need for the two services to be rationalised.

As a result of these discussions and the fall in business lost to the tunnel, the vehicular ferry from Birkenhead was reduced to one vessel and the service was suspended in July 1941, after the onset of the Second World War.

(top right) *The* **Mountwood**, *complete with wooden mainmast, seen on 29th April 1970 with the yellow/blue funnel livery of the M.P.T.A. photo: Malcolm McRonald.*
(bottom right) *Classic photograph! The* **Royal Daffodil** *in Wallasey Corporation colours in the late 1960s. The* **Manx Maid** *and the old* **Lady of Mann** *are in the background.* *photo: Gordon Ditchfield.*

Free from their previous duties, the Birkenhead "luggage boats", **Bebington** and **Oxton** (both vehicle ferries but also carrying 200 passengers and originally each costing £63,118, twin screw sets fore and aft/1925/732 gross tons) were called up for war service and fitted with large cranes on their open vehicle decks to enable them to offload aircraft and other heavy cargo being brought into the Mersey on the decks of merchant shipping. With the Birkenhead vehicular ferry service in reality permanently closed, they were both sold for scrap after the war. Their sisterships (the **Barnston** and the **Churton**) which were four years their senior, had been sold to the Dutch just prior to the war.

The Wallasey luggage boat **Liscard** also worked for the Admiralty and was fitted with a crane and used for duties similar to those of her Birkenhead counterparts.

During the war, when not on ferry or other important service, the **Hinderton** (and also other vessels on occasion) ran various cruises including some out into the river to view assembling merchant ship convoys.

At 22.20 on the last day of June, 1939, the **Upton** had closed the Rock Ferry service, for which she was originally designed. During the war she was requisitioned by the Admiralty carrying supplies and men to the various anti-aircraft defences in and around Liverpool Bay. The Wallasey ferry, **Royal Daffodil II** (1934) was not alone in being assigned the duty of standing by troopships moored in the river in case of a direct bomb hit, necessitating the speedy evacuation of troops. During the war she was engaged on ferry duties and also acted as tender and troopship for the war effort. However on the night of 8th May 1941, whilst the German Luftwaffe was blitzing Merseyside again, the **Royal Daffodil II** was alongside at Seacombe and was herself hit by a bomb, which exploded directly on her starboard side near the main engine room, causing her to sink. More than a year later on 2nd June 1942, as a result of quite a difficult salvage operation, she was refloated, fitted-out (no longer to the luxurious standards of before) and returned to the ferry service on 2nd June 1943. Thereafter she burned oil fuel. Her return enabled the older ferries **J. Farley** and **Francis Storey** to go permanently on Admiralty service.

The **J. Farley**, and the **Francis Storey** were duly taken over by the Admiralty but, still manned with their regular ferry crews, they were put to valuable work on torpedo net laying duties. The **J. Farley** was at Milford Haven and the Clyde during this period whilst the **Francis Storey** remained secretly based around Liverpool Bay.

The continuity of the cross-river link was vital and the ferry services operated throughout the war, subject to alteration and interruption by bombing, the blitzes and helping with the war effort.

Extracts from the Wallasey Corporation Ferries tolls and charges 1920.

"The Corporation are not required to carry on board their boats any goods of a dangerous nature. Failure to give proper notice and to mark any dangerous goods will render the goods liable to be thrown overboard."

(caption for pictures on page 25)
The **Royal Daffodil II** (built 1934) received a direct hit on the night of 8th May 1941, during the blitzes of Liverpool by the German Luftwaffe. The ship sank upright at her berth at Seacombe and the main blast of the explosion went straight up her funnel, thus saving some structural damage although her hull plating was ripped open. Sitting on the bottom, she quickly filled with sand and silt washing in and out with the tide and over 300 tons had to be removed during and after the salvage. Following a very difficult operation she was raised, rebuilt and returned to ferry service two years later. In the four photographs opposite, the ship is shown sunk, being rebuilt and in cruising and normal liveries. photos: Mac Fenton collection.

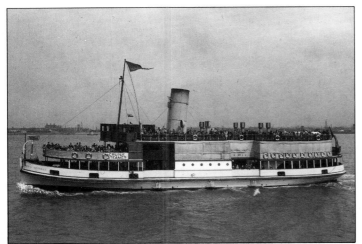

Having witnessed the end of hostilities, the ferries returned to normal working and their daily routines whilst being predictable, were certainly not dull. The vagaries of the Mersey weather with its gales, fog and even occasional ice in the river gave a certain excitement to the proceedings. Collisions, though rare, were not unheard of as ferries grappled with the tide (sometimes flowing at 7 knots) and other difficult conditions which occasionally swept them onto the landing stages, other vessels or the mud at low water.

The annals of history are laden with accounts of near misses and of evasive action taken by gallant ferry captains to keep or get their vessels out of harm's way. There was a tremendous camaraderie between the members of the ferry crews within their own fleet and reports of captains sensing danger and sounding warnings to other ferries are quite common. Clearly this alertness and dedication was instrumental in keeping the ferries out of danger and their passengers safe. However, in earlier days, there was little (if any) affection demonstrated between the crews of the Birkenhead ferries and those from Wallasey, each of whom regarded the other as its rival.

The Birkenhead Corporation ferry **Claughton** *was coal fired and steam powered throughout her life.*   *photo: Richard Danielson collection.*

Birkenhead Ferries — post war operations

After the war, the fleet of five pre-war passenger ferries operated by Birkenhead Corporation was intact, but the **Upton's** days were numbered as we shall see shortly.

The then active Birkenhead fleet comprised the **Upton** (1925/374 gross tons), **Hinderton** (1925/484 gross tons), **Thurstaston** (1930/487 gross tons), **Claughton** (1930/487 gross tons), **Bidston** (1933/487 gross tons).

All five were very similar looking ships and came from Cammell Laird's, Birkenhead. With the exception of the **Upton** (the capacity of which was 1,113 passengers) they were licensed to carry 1,433 passengers and had a length of 150 feet b.p. and a beam of almost 41 feet. The **Upton** was the smallest of the quintet and, having been designed especially for the Rock Ferry service, was a little less powerful, smaller in dimensions (length 145 feet b.p., breadth 32 feet) and tonnage than the rest. Mechanically, the few years that separated them produced some minor mechanical changes but typically, their triple expansion, steam reciprocating engines delivered 1,300 horsepower at the indicator and twin screws propelled them at about 11 knots.

The **Thurstaston** and the **Claughton** were both built under the same contract (dated 2nd December 1929) between Birkenhead Corporation and Cammell Laird & Company Limited. The price for the two ships was to be £85,690 in total, which was payable as follows: 20 per cent upon the keel being laid, 20 per cent when the ship was framed, 20 per cent after plating was complete and 20 per cent at launching. Thereafter, the remaining 15 per cent was to be paid upon delivery with the balance of 5 per cent retained for six months pending satisfactory service of the ships.

The **Bidston's** contract was signed on 8th September 1932, and as all the design work was already done for the previous ships in the class, she was somewhat less expensive at £40,675. They were all instantly recognisable as none (at the time) had navigating bridges. The Birkenhead ferries'

Since about 1890, the passenger ferries operated by Birkenhead Corporation have carried their names in distinctive script writing on their bows, whilst on their sterns the name and port of registry, Liverpool, were in ordinary lettering. The "luggage boats" did not adopt this very attractive, "freestyle" approach. However, as became apparent when trying to match the typeface for use in this book, the style has not always been uniform throughout the years. For example, compare the script as in **Overchurch** *(above) with that as in* **Claughton** *and* **Thurstaston** *on pages 26 and 30. The above photograph of the* **Overchurch** *taken in October 1991 also shows a mistake in the Roman numerals which indicate the ship's draft marks jumping from eight feet (VIII) to eleven feet (XI instead of IX).* photo: Richard Danielson

belting was protected by distinctive, if ragged looking, fenders made of rope matting and their names were carried in fancy script writing on their bows, rather than printed Roman characters. Their design clearly inherited many of the generic features of the earlier Birkenhead ferries in that they all had lofty funnels, hoarse sounding steam whistles, massive beams and belting, yet none had superstructure on their large, open upper deck. In place of the traditional engine room ventilator cowls, they had wooden box structures housing the necessary vents.

One of the exciting things about travelling in the days of the old steam ferries was to sit on the bench seating around the main deck. Here it was possible to peer under the seats through the engine room sidelights to see the stokers hard at work with their black faces glistening with sweat, shovelling coal into the furnaces for raising boiler steam. The triple expansion steam reciprocating machinery was beautifully smooth in operation and far quieter than today's internal combustion engines.

On the upper deck, in the absence of a navigating bridge, the officers worked from a small central wheelhouse above which the ship's bell was mounted, or side cab (not much larger than a telephone kiosk), protected only by a perfunctory notice warning passengers not to talk to officers whilst the vessel was underway.

The earlier closure of the Rock Ferry service had rendered the *Upton* virtually redundant and after the War she was sold by Birkenhead Corporation for further use on the South Coast arriving at Southampton in May 1946. Her new owners were the Southampton, Isle of Wight and South of England Royal Mail Steam Packet Company Limited, more commonly known as "Red Funnel Steamers" and they operated ferries to the Isle of Wight from Southampton, excursions, tugs and tendering facilities for visiting liners. It was intended that the *Upton* would help swell their fleet but

as she had no vehicle capacity, her main operations were expected to be the popular excursions to and from Ryde, and other trips based on Poole and elsewhere.

Complete with her Birkenhead name still in script on her bow (there being several villages in Hampshire and Dorset thus named), but with side mounted lifeboats, new dining saloon and a magnificent new navigating bridge and wheelhouse, the *Upton* took up service. Her bell survived the transformation and for the rest of her days, was hung proudly on the forward end of her newly rebuilt teak superstructure.

However it quickly became clear that the beamy stalwart from the Mersey was less than efficient at her new tasks due to her great breadth and rather slow speed. By then she rarely managed to exceed 10 knots. Nor was she very popular or suitable for tendering as she had nowhere designed for the carriage of vehicles and bulky luggage for shipment to or from the liners.

The **Upton** at Southampton after her sale to Red Funnel Steamers in 1946.   photo: L. Speller.

She was withdrawn after just five years' work and apart from a brief, unsuccessful period of trials to see if she could take on any of the Company's towage duties, remained at Northam until 1953 when she was broken up at Pollock Brown's Yard.

Northam was something of a Mecca for the author in the 1950s and 1960s and it was often possible to find several paddlers and other excursion ships and ferries resting there together, laid up under overhaul at Thornycroft's or just temporarily unemployed.

Mostly, the ships of each Corporation's fleet stayed within their own control. However, the **Hinderton** was, for several seasons in the early 1950s, to be found on charter to Wallasey Corporation for their Seacombe and New Brighton runs. She also carried out some interesting cruises including one in 1948, when she sailed towards Runcorn and Widnes by navigating the now disused upper reaches of the River Mersey, rather than the Manchester ship canal close-by.

At the same period, Birkenhead Corporation ferries were looking at the possibility of running a service from Woodside to New Brighton but concluded that such an innovation was likely to loose money.

While Wallasey Corporation were experimenting with the small **Wallasey Belle** which they had bought from J. Bolson & Son Ltd., it is not generally known that their Birkenhead counterparts were also considering smaller, more economic tonnage. Bolsons, the Poole based shipbuilder and operator having successfully dealt with Wallasey Corporation in 1949, then contacted Birkenhead ferries department through their brokers to see if they might be interested in a ship Bolsons had on the stocks under construction. The ship was the **Bournemouth Belle** and the General Manager at Birkenhead ferries requested sight of the plans and specifications. However, he decided that the new ship was of too light construction for the Woodside ferry service, particularly in

heavy winter weather.

In March 1955 the Transport Manager reported to the Municipal Transport Committee at Birkenhead that a survey done on the **Hinderton** revealed that her hull plating had worn very thin and would prove costly to restore. In the same report, the hope was expressed that Wallasey and Birkenhead might share the responsibility of providing a standby boat, thus reducing the overall combined fleets by one ship. Wallasey responded by agreeing in principle but with the added rider that they could not guarantee that any spare ship of theirs would necessarily be available when needed!

After running the night service, the **Hinderton** ran her last trip at 05.40 on 13th May 1956. She was then retired from the Birkenhead ferry service and laid up for a long time. She was towed away for scrapping in Antwerp in September 1958.

Three years later in July 1961, the **Thurstaston** left the Mersey destined further work carrying cargo for her new owners in Holland on the myriad of inland waterways there. However, it is thought that she was broken up in 1965, never having commenced the new service.

The **Bidston** was also surplus to requirements and went on charter to the Harbour Commissioners at Cork (where she was then registered) during 1960/61, prior to being broken up there in 1962.

By the Spring of 1960, Birkenhead Corporation had taken delivery of both of its new Dartmouth-built diesel ferries which were named **Mountwood** and **Woodchurch**, leaving just the **Claughton** as the last Birkenhead example from the pre-war, coal fired, steam powered, ferry era. Their third new ship, the **Overchurch**, was completed on Merseyside and arrived two years later. These three ferries are still actively in service on the Mersey and full details of their careers can be found later in the book.

The **Claughton**, having become the last steamer in the

Birkenhead fleet, ran her last sailings at the end of 1961. At the time, she was reported as being rather the worse for wear. She was laid up in the Morpeth Dock next to the Wallasey ferry, **St. Hilary** (ex **Royal Daffodil II**, built 1934). On 21st September 1962, they were both towed away simultaneously by the tug **Ocean Bull**, for scrapping in Ghent. The Liverpool Echo of the day carried an emotive photograph showing duty ferryman, Mr. Keith Smith waving farewell to the two ferries from New Brighton landing stage.

(top right) *The* **Claughton**, *complete with spars for sun deck awnings. The trouble is, that whilst everyone can remember the spars, few can actually remember the awnings!* photo: Malcolm McRonald.

(bottom right) *Third of the Birkenhead Corporation quintet, the* **Thurstaston** *is arriving at Liverpool landing stage on 18th April 1959.* photo: Malcolm McRonald.

(below) *Deck view aboard the* **Bidston** *on the other side of the Irish sea whilst on charter to Cork Harbour Commissioners, who were awaiting the delivery of their new passenger carrying tender. Note the absence of deck seating and the arrival of the two, large lifeboats.* photo: Malcolm McRonald.

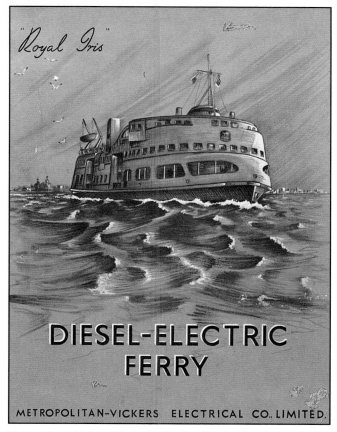

*Metropolitan-Vickers Limited of Trafford Park, Manchester, (where the author's father qualified) were justly proud of the electrical layout of the diesel-electric powered **Royal Iris**. This illustration is from the front cover of their prospectus of the ship, inviting enquiries from other shipowners.*

Wallasey Ferries — post war operations

The Seacombe vehicular service survived the war but it soon ended consequent upon the expiration of an operating agreement with the Great Western Railway. Of the ships, the Southampton built **Liscard** (1921/ 734 gross tons) was sold for further service (still as a crane ship) in 1946 and for about the next twenty years found work in Denmark and Holland. She realised £10,000 for Wallasey Corporation and left the Mersey on 9th November 1946 for delivery by her ferry crew under Captain Mason. Her sistership, the **Leasowe** (1921/ 734 gross tons) was laid up and sold two years later for breaking up probably at Troon, Ayrshire but some old records say that she was towed to Thos Ward & Son Ltd. Preston on 9th August 1948, first. The scrap price of just £1,850 that she realised, is not in doubt. Until the closure of the service, the remaining Wallasey ferry on the vehicular service to Seacombe was the newest and largest "luggage boat", the **Perch Rock**. The final vehicle carrying ferry ran in March 1947 after which date the service ceased altogether.

Following the war, the active fleet of vessels operated by the County Borough of Wallasey (owned by "The Mayor, Alderman and Burgesses of the County Borough of Wallasey") was thus:

J. Farley (1922/464 gross tons), **Francis Storey** (1922/ 464 gross tons), **Wallasey** (1927/606 gross tons), **Marlowe** (1927/606 gross tons), **Perch Rock** (vehicle ferry 1929/766 gross tons), **Royal Iris II** (1932/607 gross tons), **Royal Daffodil II** (1934/ 591 gross tons).

The ferries used to run all through the night but at reduced frequency and at an increased tariff. Before the days of V.H.F. radio, during really quiet periods in the middle of the night, the ferry would lie at Seacombe or Liverpool and cross the river once in a while to see if anyone was waiting at the other side. If no one was there, the ship would simply

The Wallasey "luggage boat" **Liscard** was on Admiralty service during the Second World War. Note the crane built on her deck for lifting aircraft etc. from the decks of merchant shipping anchored in the river. She is seen here after the war in the Egerton Dock at Birkenhead, laid-up awaiting a buyer. In peacetime, as well as being a vehicle ferry, she occasionally ran special cruises and helped out with busy passenger sailings. She was not renowned for her passenger comforts!
photo: Capt. Dennis Titherington collection.

(Above)
The Wallasey ferry **J. Farley** *had a long and varied life.*
photo: Tom Rayner.

(Top right)
The **Marlowe**, *sistership of the* **Wallasey**, *is seen here on 11th May 1957.*   *photo: Malcolm McRonald.*

(Bottom right)
The **Wallasey** *is seen here very early in her career, in service on the Mersey during the late summer of 1927. She was built by Caledon Shipbuilding and Engineering Co. Ltd, and was launched at Dundee on 31st May 1927, (Yard No. 306). Capt. T. Potter delivered her to the Mersey where she arrived on 16th July 1927. Her sistership, the* **Marlowe**, *was launched from the same yard on 29th June 1927 (Yard No. 307) and was delivered on 26th August 1927.*
photo: Caledon Shipyard Archives, Dundee.

*The **Woodchurch** in Clarence dry-dock Liverpool on 12th October 1983. It is easy to see that she was in quite a dilapidated state when the decision was taken (see page 60) to bring her back into service after nearly three years laid-up and being cannibalised to help keep her sisters supplied with spare parts. Note the separate central wheelhouse and sidecabs which were plated in during her 1990 rebuilding. photo: Gordon Ditchfield.*

glide slowly past or perhaps come alongside making fast with just one loop of the bow rope. However, on 1st January 1948, the night fare structure was abolished and all fares were thereafter the same. The next year on 14th May 1949, cheap evening return tickets on the New Brighton run were introduced to try to encourage extra traffic. For comparison the following (single) fares were in operation at the dates stated. Total passengers carried are also shown.

	Seacombe	Egremont	New Brighton	Passengers
1918	1 penny	2 pence	3 pence	31,797,271
1923	3 pence	4 pence	6 pence	25,749,455
1952	4 pence	n/a	9 pence	16,443,065

The sisters, **Francis Storey** and **J. Farley** were built at the Ailsa Shipbuilding & Engineering Company at Troon and were named after Chairmen of the Ferries' Committee. Sadly, both gentlemen died before the vessels were delivered and therefore, as a mark of respect, for their first year in service, each ship carried a four inch wide purple mourning band, painted on the outside of the bulwarks.

They were the regular Egremont/New Brighton boats from 1928 onwards, prior to which they were the mainstay of the Seacombe ferry. They were also very popular on river cruises for which the **Francis Storey** received a new livery of grey hull and buff funnel. After Admiralty service (see page 24) they were reconditioned, and the **J. Farley** was converted to burn oil fuel (for which they had both been designed almost since inception) and returned to peace time ferry duties in 1946. In reality they were becoming obsolete and when their time was up in 1951 and 1952 respectively, they were replaced with the state of the art diesel powered ships, named **Leasowe** and **Egremont**.

The **Francis Storey** went first on 8th February 1951, for the princely sum of £7,500 and renamed **Killarney**, spent another eight years with Cork Harbour Commissioners. There she was in the company of her erstwhile fleetmates, the famous **Royal Iris** (1906) and the **John Joyce** (sold by Wallasey Corporation on 3rd November 1936 for £2,450) which by then had been renamed **Shandon**. As the **Killarney**, the former **Francis Storey** was finally sold for £6,120 in 1960 and was broken up by Shirling & Sons, at their scrapyard near Cork. Her place was taken briefly by the chartered Birkenhead ferry **Bidston** until Cork Harbour Commissioners had their new 1,000 passenger ship, the **Cill Airne** delivered in 1962.

In January 1952, the **J. Farley** was sold for £12,000 through brokers, to the Admiralty Underwater Weapons Establishment, for experimental work at Portland. For this, she was towed to Weymouth where Cosens & Co, once the operators of a well known fleet of south coast paddle steamers, removed her engines and made the ship ready for her new tasks. This experimental work was very much the vogue at the time, witnessed by the fact that the Caledonian Steam Packet Company ship **Duchess of Argyll** (1906/594 gross tons) ended her days in much the same way, also in 1952.

Replaced in 1971 at the Admiralty, what remained of the **J. Farley** then passed into the hands of Mr Don Hickman whose unconsummated plans to have Husbands Shipyard convert her (and some say, even operate her again) for use in some role on the Thames, appear to have faltered. Don Hickman also had a brief encounter with ownership of the **Princess Elizabeth**, a paddle steamer owned by the Southampton Company that had purchased the former Birkenhead ferry, **Upton** in 1946.

Years later, in 1985, in a planned "ferry spectacular", there was serious discussion for M.P.T.E. to buy back the hulk of the **J. Farley** and to rebuild and restore her as a genuine museum ship. Unfortunately, the ship had been broken up by the time that the plan came close to fruition.

Five years after the arrival of the **J. Farley** and the **Francis Storey**, two more new ferries were delivered for the

October 1991 found the **Overchurch** *and the* **Woodchurch** *in dock at Birkenhead at the ferries' regular berth at Duke Street Bridge. Both ships were looking "spick and span" and were a credit to Mac Fenton, and his colleagues who were carrying out the work.*
photo: Richard Danielson.

Wallasey fleet. These were named **Wallasey** and **Marlowe** respectively and came from the Dundee shipyard of Caledon Shipbuilding and Engineering Company Limited. The **Wallasey** arrived on the Mersey on 16th July 1927, followed by the **Marlowe** on 26th August 1927, both were delivered by Captain T. Potter. The first in the fleet with cruiser sterns, and with a breadth of 48 feet and length of 151 feet b.p., their aspect ratio was comparable to that of the "luggage boats". With twin screws again and steam reciprocating, triple expansion machinery suitably uprated for their extra workload, the new ferries also had the new Flettner system of twin rudders aft to facilitate close quarters manoeuvring. Their underwater hull designs were finalised after tests were carried out at the National Physical Laboratory, Teddington. Theirs was the final basic design concept of the remaining steam powered Mersey ferries. Also, as if to perpetuate the species, their genes were obvious in many more ferries, some built much later, including the post war diesel engined Mersey ferries and the Southern Railway motorships **Brading**, **Southsea** and **Shanklin**.

Originally the **Wallasey** and the **Marlowe** were coal fired and proved to be popular good-looking, efficient movers of large numbers of passengers. Each could carry 2,233 passengers and their boilers consumed 9 tons of coal per day steaming at 12 knots. By comparison, their immediate predecessors carried just over 1,600 passengers at 11 knots and consumed 11 tons of coal per day. Lloyds Register shows that they were equipped to burn oil fuel from 1939, but it was not until their post-war refits that the conversion was actually effected.

With their arrival on the Seacombe service, the two older ships moved to the New Brighton station although a certain amount of interchanging was still to occur. The **Marlowe** was first to reach the end of her life and at the end of 1958 after 31 years' service, realised £6,000 when she was sold for

scrapping by the British Iron & Steel Corporation.

The **Wallasey** had the distinction of becoming the last steam powered Mersey ferry and she remained in service until Whitsun 1963. She was in steam again for the hoped for August Bank Holiday rush of that year, which, on account of the inclement weather failed to materialise and she stood down without carrying a single passenger. She was sold in January 1964 for £5,150 after which she was towed away for scrapping at Ghent by the famous shipbreakers, Van Heyghen Frères and thus she left the Mersey on 20th February 1964.

The **Perch Rock** (named after the fortress at New Brighton marking the entrance to the River Mersey) was the last "luggage boat" built for the vehicular service from Seacombe. Her length was 144 feet b.p. and she was 50 feet in breadth. Like her passenger carrying consorts the **Wallasey** and the **Marlowe**, the very beamy **Perch Rock** was also built at Caledon Shipbuilding and Engineering Co Ltd, Dundee and had similar main engines. When car carrying terminated in 1947, following minor alterations to make her (marginally) better suited to her passenger carrying duties, the **Perch Rock** started a new phase of her career and continued in service as a relief passenger ship for a further six years. There was even talk of her being refitted as a "new super luxury passenger/cruise ferry", but talk was all it ever was. Perhaps surprisingly, all the Wallasey "luggage boats" held full passenger certificates (**Perch Rock** 1,600 passengers, **Leasowe** and **Liscard** 1,788 each). Despite their almost total lack of facilities, they were occasionally used to provide special cruises and there is a good story told on Merseyside of the day when almost 1,000 people on one such trip, queued all afternoon for the single toilet situated right aft on the **Liscard**!

The paucity of proper accommodation aboard the **Perch Rock** must have made her quite unsuitable for these new duties although, in common with some of the other ferries,

Three views of the last Wallasey "luggage boat", the **Perch Rock**, *which was built by Caledon Shipbuilding and Engineering and Co Ltd, and was launched at Dundee on 6th February 1929.*
(above) On her trials, bedecked with bunting and smoking well!
(right) Making ready for her delivery voyage from Dundee. Note the coal, stacked in bags on deck, for consumption on the long trip.
photo: Caledon Shipyard Archives, Dundee.

Two official postcards depicting the futuristic looking **Royal Iris** *as she looked for about the first half of her career. Originally, as shown in the (top) John Nicholson picture, the green hull paint stopped at the belting but later (below), it was raised one strake higher.*
photos: George Danielson collection.

a canvas awning was erected which would have provided passengers with some minimal protection from the elements. Buoyancy type seating was also spread around her massive former vehicle deck providing basic comfort for her passengers for whom a voyage on the **Perch Rock** must have been something of a culture shock! However, she was not without her followers and was appreciated for her noticeable powerful bursts of speed, if not for the quality of passenger comfort.

She was sold on 17th December 1953, for £8,800 (which yielded £8,120 after brokers' commission) to Scandinavian interests who renamed her **Betula** and converted her into a freight train ferry for the carriage of sugar beet between Bergkvara and Morbylanga on Oland Island. In 1954 she was reported to have been converted back to car carrying between Korsor and Nyborg and a year later received a new glass and teak fronted bridge and a large passenger promenade deck. Gradually she was changed beyond all possible recognition except for her (original looking) wooden wheelhouse. Immediately, she was to be found operating as a passenger ferry between Helsingborg and Helsingor and started the famous Scandinavian Ferry Line. In 1968, she had the prefix "**I**" added to her name to allow it to be used by Linjebuss, her owners' new **Betula**, then about to be introduced. She was finally laid up in 1971 and sold to AB Skanska Cementgjutenet of Malmo. At Helsingborg, her conversion for use as a working cement platform commenced on 10th January 1972 where the superstructure that had been added for her "second life" in Scandinavia, was removed and much of her machinery was retained for further use. For the purposes of this book, she ceased to be a "ship" at that time.

Two fine new large passenger ships were added to the fleet in 1932 and 1934 respectively just after the old **Royal Iris** and **Royal Daffodil** of Zeebrugge fame were sold.

As mentioned in the chapter dealing with their daring

raid in the First World War, the old **Royal Iris** (dating from 1906) was the first to go and she was replaced by a ship of the same name but with the suffix "**II**' added. The new ship was handsome and the first ferry on the River Mersey to have three decks complete with awning on the top sundeck, abaft the funnel. Completed in 1932 by Harland & Wolff at Govan with engines from nearby D & W Henderson at their Meadowside Works, Glasgow, the **Royal Iris II** had the most elaborate interior of any ferry with a beautifully panelled, Tudor style, main passenger saloon. Difficulty in obtaining the right coal made her run more and more slowly and in the end, she had to miss the occasional sailing to "catch up" with the timetable. Whilst she had clearly come from a similar mould as the **Wallasey** and the **Marlowe**, with a passenger certificate for 2,024, she carried slightly fewer people.

In 1947, the ship was renamed by simply dropping the suffix "**II**' from her name as by then, her predecessor was working in Cork and had been renamed **Blarney**. In the end, the ship had to yield up her illustrious title in readiness for the arrival of the brand new, diesel-electric cruise ship, being built at Wm. Denny's famous Dumbarton shipyard. To this end, the 1932 built **Royal Iris** was again renamed in 1950, this time becoming the **St. Hilary** (after one of the wards of the Borough of Wallasey) and remained thus until her departure from the Mersey in 1956. Still a reasonably young and active ship, for £12,000 she was disposed of to new Dutch owners Stolk NV, and was partially dismantled at Hendrik Ido Ambacht, near Dordrecht. Her hull and what remained of her machinery were bought by N.V. Rotterdamsche Tramweg Maats on 12th September 1957 and she was towed to Verschure NV Dockyard, Amsterdam where two new diesel 550 bhp engines were fitted and the ship was completely rebuilt for the carriage of 40 vehicles. Converted at a cost of £150,000 the ship returned to service between Hellvoetsluis and Middleharnis in the autumn of

The **Royal Iris** heads for the Flower Festival site in August 1984. photo: Richard Danielson.

The **Royal Iris**, loading for her afternoon cruise on 31st July 1982. photo: Richard Danielson.

1957 carrying the name **Haringvliet**. Fourteen years later, she changed hands again and was renamed **Schellingerland** for further service, this time between Terschelling and Harlingen in Holland's Waddenland.

Two years junior to the **Royal Iris II**, the **Royal Daffodil II** was built at Birkenhead by Cammell Laird & Co Limited, Shipbuilders and Engineers in 1934 for a contract price of £44,790. She too was fitted-out to a very high standard with teak and oak used extensively in her passenger accommodation. Her main engine boilers produced superheated steam which brought about further operational economies, enabling average daily coal consumption to be reduced to just 7 3/4 tons. She was instrumental in popularising dance cruises on the ferries and after the war (see pages 24/25) was to run many successful pleasure trips, taking on a new white and yellow livery for the purpose.

In January 1956, a watchman aboard the ship in the Morpeth dock found the main engine room valve open in what is thought to have been a deliberate attempt to sink the vessel. In the event, whilst she had taken water aboard and was sinking by the stern, her perilous condition was realised just in time and rectified. By 1957, Wallasey Ferries had a new large diesel ferry on the stocks at Port Glasgow and the old **Royal Daffodil II** was renamed **St. Hilary** (which, as we saw in the case of the **Royal Iris** is the temporary or reserve name kept for such purposes) in readiness for the coming of the new ship which was to take over the name.

As the **St. Hilary**, she remained operational for a further four years mainly doing summer relief work with her old fleetmate, the **Wallasey**. Finally laid up in the Morpeth dock and unused for months, she and the Birkenhead steam ferry, **Claughton**, were towed away together on 21st September 1962, by the tug **Ocean Bull**, bound for the ship breakers.

On 17th November 1949, Wallasey Corporation broke with tradition and having purchased the former Fairmile motor launch named **Channel Belle** from J. Bolson & Son Ltd. for £13,500, Captain Mason delivered the ship to Merseyside.

Like so many other ex Royal Naval rescue launches which became available soon after the War (almost seven hundred were reportedly constructed), she was built of double diagonal mahogany on oak frames, the whole hull, the bottom of which was sheathed in copper, being fastened together with over two tons of copper nails. She had been built at Leigh on Sea in 1944, towards the end of the hostilities and was converted by Bolsons at Poole for passenger work after which, based at Bournemouth on the south coast, she had been running short cruises carrying up to 250 passengers. The smart little twin screw vessel had two 6 cylinder diesel engines made by Gray Marine Motor Company, Detroit, Michigan and they could propel her at over 10 knots. She

The **Wallasey Belle** *whilst pretty, was really too small for comfort. photo: Gordon Ditchfield collection.*

had two almost flat topped funnels, was 108 feet long b.p. and had a gross tonnage of 126 tons. During her short time with Wallasey Corporation, she had a number of different liveries including green hull, black hull, cream hull, yellow funnels with and without green bands. In April 1950, she was renamed **Wallasey Belle** and for three years was used for cruising and ferry work. She was considered suitable for the night ferry traffic which was very light between the hours of midnight and 06.00. She was really too small for cruising and in all but the calmest weather must have been very lively, especially off New Brighton where the estuary is quite exposed to the fury of the Irish Sea. On 30th November 1953, she was sold for just £1,250 to Mr A P Martin of Heswall (some records suggest Australian interests) and then renamed with her original peacetime name, **Channel Belle**.

Readers may also like to know, that almost half a century after their building, several other ex-wartime "Fairmiles" are still giving stalwart service as pleasure craft in British waters. These include the two lovely **Western Lady** ferries based at Torquay and the **Golden Galleon** at Great Yarmouth.

Over a century ago, the famous Wm. Denny & Bros. Dumbarton shipyard constructed several early Mersey ferries but in December 1950, they excelled themselves by producing the twin screw, diesel-electric ship **Royal Iris** for Wallasey Corporation. Yard No. 1448, the **Royal Iris** ran her trials on the famous Skelmorlie mile on the Clyde on 24th April 1951, and was delivered to the Mersey on 28th April 1951. She was by far the largest and most commodious vessel ever built for the all year round service from Liverpool to Seacombe and the summer service to New Brighton. Her gross tonnage was 1,234 tons and she was 160 feet overall in length and 48 feet in breadth. The "Iris" was also to have the dual role of being principal summer cruise boat and for this, she was designed with a Class III passenger certificate to enable her to sail on short excursions to sea. Class III certificates are generally only valid between April (Easter if earlier) and October and for voyages within the period of one hour before sunrise to one hour after sunset. No Class III passenger carrying voyage may normally exceed 70 nautical miles in length nor take the ship more than 18 miles from the United Kingdom coast. Originally the **Royal Iris** could carry 2,296 passengers on her Class V (smooth water) certificate and 1,000 when running on her seasonal Class III certificate.

Outwardly, she differed from any other ship and was very sleek above the waterline, resembling a large waterbus. She carried the Borough coat of arms proudly on the front of her streamlined superstructure, until the ultimate merging of the Wallasey and Birkenhead ferry fleets. Over the years, other authors have said some unkind things about her

Occasionally, when circumstances permit, the ferries have been beached at Egremont (also at New Brighton in years gone by) for underwater attention between the tides. Here the **Royal Iris** *is receiving the treatment.*   *photo: Ray Pugh.*

The **Egremont** *seen on 12th October 1974 in the colours of the Merseyside Passenger Transport Authority.*   *photo: Malcolm McRonald.*

*The extra top hamper of the **Royal Daffodil** is quite evident in this view dated 14th June 1975 as is the unhappy visual effect of her receiving the green funnel livery matching the Corporation controlled buses!*

photo: Malcolm McRonald.

(top left) The **Leasowe's** *troublesome propellers.*

(top right) The **Leasowe's** *funnel and illuminated name box.*

(bottom left) The **Egremont** *is seen here on 20th January 1952, fitting out at Philip & Sons Ltd. with her wheelhouse sidecabs under construction. The occasion was also the launch day for the coaster* **Lady Sylvia.**

(bottom right) The **Leasowe** *in dry-dock at Dartmouth after her trials and having had her propellers removed and adjusted for better performance. all photos: Richard Danielson collection.*

Whilst compiling this book, the author was able to purchase the entire collection of official launching and trials shipping photographs taken by photographer N. Horne of Totnes, Devon. His business has now been taken over and is known as The Portrait Studio. Some of the collection appear on pages 44, 46 and 57 herein.

appearance, but for those of us with whom she shared much of our lives, we could see little actually wrong with her unusual, futuristic lines. Her hull under water was designed to facilitate instant manoeuvring and control in the often crowded shipping lanes of the River Mersey. She had also to be capable of withstanding the gales which regularly sweep the Mersey Estuary, especially in the winter months. Nevertheless, despite all this careful planning, there were occasions in her career when she had difficulty getting off the Landing Stage in strong, beam winds. Mechanically, she was very advanced, particularly when compared with her remaining steam powered consorts, the **Wallasey**, the **Marlowe** and the **Royal Daffodil II**.

The **Royal Iris** was built with four diesel generator sets connected to two Metropolitan Vickers electrical propulsion motors which, between them, could produce a total of 1,460 horsepower if required. The beauty of the system was that she could run almost as well on just three generators and power was instantly controllable from the bridge. The "Metrovick" experience had been gained over many years and included the diesel-electric installations in David MacBrayne Limited's vessel **Loch Fyne** and the two Firth of Forth ferries, **Queen Margaret** and **Robert the Bruce**. In their publicity letter at the time of the order being placed for the **Royal Iris**, Metropolitan Vickers boasted (not without good cause) that electrical repairs on the **Loch Fyne** had cost less than £25.00 in twenty years of running!

Originally she had a bright yellow and green livery which was later modified by raising the green hull paint one strake higher. In 1971/2 this later gave way to plain blue and white followed by all the colours of the Union Jack for her sailings in connection with the Liverpool Flower Festival of 1984/85, which colourful image she retained until the beginning of her final season. For use with her Class III passenger certificate, she originally had a pair of large, side slung lifeboats which were removed in the 1971/2 winter face-lift. In about 1954, to accord with new navigation light requirements affecting ships longer than 150 feet the **Royal Iris**, **St. Hilary**, **Royal Daffodil**, **Wallasey** and **Marlowe** all had a mainmast fitted upon which to carry the new, forward facing white light. The length of 150 feet was quite critical as the ferries were either longer or shorter than this, depending whether they were measured "overall" (o.a.) or "between perpendiculars" (b.p.).

Different interpretation of the new regulations affected ferries again in 1966 and some that had not had them earlier, had mainmasts fitted then. Later, some wooden mainmasts gave way to steel ones following which it was realised that the regulations did not apply after all! The remaining mainmasts were then removed.

Latterly, the **Royal Iris** sailed only with a Class V licence for 1,200 passengers, but rarely carried more than half that number.

As a cruise ship, she gained the nickname of "the fish and chip boat" or "the booze boat" on account of the large volumes of food and drink consumed on such trips. At different times, she was also marketed as a "Great Summer Sail" and "The Mersey Pirate". She had a large area for dining and drinking and a spacious dance floor. Midway through her career, the sum of £68,000 was provided for the creation of a new steak bar and superb dining area capable of accommodating 150 passengers. This was in place of the original "fish and chip café" layout which was incorporated in her original design. All the work was carried out at Bootle by Harland and Wolff at the end of 1971. Her passenger accommodation was large by Mersey ferry standards and there was room for over two thousand passengers undercover!

Gradually, New Brighton fell from favour and for the last quarter of a century, its demise was a tragedy, if not a something of a scandal. The last ferry operated on 26th September 1971, with heavy silting of the berth having made

(above) The **Leasowe** boarded up and ready for her delivery voyage to Merseyside. She had cost £142,700 to build.

(top right) The **Leasowe** is seen here streaking across Start Bay on her trials, on 1st November 1951.

(bottom right) The moment of truth as the **Egremont** enters the water for the first time when she was launched at Dartmouth on 10th December 1951.

photos: Richard Danielson collection.

its use impossible on certain occasions in the previous few years. The debate continued as to whether the route should or could be saved. In the end, the battle was lost and the pier was finally demolished in 1978 as the "powers that be" decided that it had no future for pleasure activities.

On 21st June 1977, the **Royal Iris** had the honour of carrying Her Majesty Queen Elizabeth and His Royal Highness, the Duke of Edinburgh on their memorable Jubilee Mersey Review. Early in her career, the **Royal Iris's** most distant seaward destination from Liverpool was to the Bar Lightship, 14 miles north west out to sea. Sailing inland, in the later part of her career she traversed the Manchester Ship Canal on occasions, carrying cruise passengers. The ship canal starts at Eastham Lock, 19 miles inland from the Bar and is over 35 miles in length before reaching Manchester. In the 1980s, she also found useful employment as a floating restaurant, for which task she moored at the Pier Head and was marketed as the "Quarterdeck", providing lunchtime refreshment for Liverpool's city folk and tourists.

Her original Lloyds classification included the perceived likelihood of some sailings from Liverpool to Barrow and Holyhead to Caernarvon using her Class III certificate. However, since her delivery from Scotland, the only occasion the **Royal Iris** has ever gone outside the Mersey or Liverpool Bay was in April and May 1985 when she was sent southwards on a publicity drive for Merseyside. At that time she sailed all the way round Land's End, on to London and under Tower Bridge, berthing adjacent to H.M.S. **Belfast**. Some say that the effort was really too much for her but nevertheless, she accomplished the 1,500 mile trip without incident and returned home safely and triumphantly a month later! Over the years as she grew older, much slower and more expensive to maintain, the **Royal Iris** saw less and less regular work. With the closure of the New Brighton service and as the popularity of eating, drinking and dancing on long river cruises waned, the operations of the ship declined in direct proportion.

She served the people of Merseyside and its visitors loyally for 40 years during which period, with that one notable exception, she remained faithful to the ferry routes and cruising for which she was designed.

Her last full season was the summer of 1990. Repainted mainly white, with a blue hull, the **Royal Iris** was present and very busy on 24th July 1990, when the Cunard flagship **Queen Elizabeth 2** visited the Mersey for the first time. Sadly, the writing was on the wall for the **Royal Iris**, and with a major survey due, the necessary funds (thought to run to millions of pounds) could not be found to secure her future in isolation. As we shall see a little later, substantial money was provided to ensure the long term future of the Mersey ferries in general and for supplementary cruising too.

In her 40th year of operations and by then a rather tired old lady, the **Royal Iris** ran a farewell evening cruise on 12th January 1991, prior to being taken out of service and laid up pending a report into her future. After lying almost forgotten in Birkenhead on a minimum care and maintenance basis, she set sail once more on 21st April 1991, with a special one day licence from the Department of Transport, granted to enable her to carry 600 people on the 73rd anniversary trip to commemorate the Zeebrugge raid of 1918.

The report into her future came in August 1991 and gave little hope for continued use of the vessel as a ferry due to the great costs involved in bringing her up to modern standards and getting her through survey. She was costing over £70,000 per year just to remain tied up. With no obvious suitable static career for her either, on Friday 16th August 1991, the **Royal Iris** was placed in the hands of ship brokers, S.C. Chambers Limited of Liverpool for an asking price of £100,000 which is well in excess of her scrap value. A number of interested parties inspected the ship including one who wished to use her out in Hong Kong. In the end she was sold in November 1991 for use as a floating nightclub owned by "Mr. Smith's Nightclub".

To replace the **J. Farley** and the **Francis Storey**, two useful ferries were built for Wallasey Corporation by Philip & Son Limited at Dartmouth. Named **Leasowe** and **Egremont**, the 566 gross ton ships were brought into service in 1951 and 1952 respectively. Both were delivered in traditional livery and (like the **Royal Iris** before them and the later **Royal Daffodil II**) carried their names in illuminated boxes by the bridge. With three decks given over to passengers, they were licensed to carry 1,472/1,475 respectively on their Class V passenger certificates (latterly 1,200) and 692 when cruising. The Class V (smooth water) certificate covered sailings above Rock Lighthouse on the river and later, this was subdivided between long and short voyages.

Their cruising was permitted using a Class IV certificate (partially smooth waters) which was for sailings within the line Formby Point to Hilbre Point. They introduced catering on the cross river services. Physically, they were handsome craft, a little smaller than their peers, having principal dimensions of 145 feet extreme length and 34 feet breadth.

Power came from twin Crossley two stroke diesels developing some 1,280 horsepower. Each engine was direct drive and reversing with no clutch or gearboxes. The captain had control of main engine speed but the engineers controlled engine movements by responding to telegraph signals from the bridge. Engine movements were effected by stopping and injecting compressed air into the cylinders to run the engine in reverse. Despite the complexity of manoeuvring in the Mersey, it was found that this was a very reliable and efficient method of controlling the main engines. Many of the ferry masters record that, in their view, the **Leasowe** was the easiest of all the ferries to handle.

The **Leasowe** ran her main trials on 1st November 1951, and made 14.12 knots on the fastest of her six runs across Start Bay, Devon. However, propeller problems caused interesting exchanges of letters between Crossley Bros, Philip & Sons and Wallasey Corporation. After much contemplation and various adjustments to the original propellers, they were finally replaced with a pair 3 inches less in diameter. These allowed the engines to run up to full revolutions (370 r.p.m.) without overloading which had been limiting the previous maximum to 325 revolutions. Achieving 13.38 knots, the **Egremont** was a little slower on her trials which she ran on 27th March 1952, but this was not surprising as the sea was very rough with 10 feet waves reported. It was noted by Philip & Sons (with some satisfaction) that the foredeck remained dry throughout the whole trials period, despite the inclement weather. In the end, the **Egremont** had new propellers fitted too, but her original ones (the starboard one of which had been altered to be one inch less in diameter than the port one to match the engines' performance) lasted until January 1961, at which time Scimitar propellers were fitted in dry-dock at Birkenhead.

The **Leasowe** left her birthplace on the River Dart on the evening of 17th November 1951, to begin her delivery voyage. She spent the night as an unusual visitor at Brixham Harbour from where she departed at 09.00 on the 18th, arriving at New Brighton without incident at 22.32 on 19th November 1951. The **Egremont's** delivery voyage started at 19.00 on 31st March 1952, and she was safely tied up at New Brighton at 05.30 on 2nd April. Her cost was £144,500.

The two twins became the mainstay of the fleet and were to be found working on both the Wallasey and New Brighton routes (and cruises) in all weathers. Their deck hands who had responsibility for the forward rope had a problem when mooring the ship. Access to the bow mooring rope and bollards was gained by either walking through the main passenger saloon (difficult enough when the ship was full) or by "holding on tight" and walking along the rubbing strake on the outside of the bulwarks. This was considered to be a design weakness and all later ferries reverted to having saloons which were not the full breadth of the ship. Clearly the latter practice was risky and unacceptable but being a quick expedient, was to be seen on many occasions. Until 1982, a similar task had to be performed by the Chief Officers of the old Manx boats who had to climb out over the front of the bridge and superstructure, stretch across onto the rigging of the foremast and then make a hasty descent to the fo'c'sle to handle the bow ropes.

When the **Leasowe** was brand new thus sporting a complete and very expensive set of ropes, one young student acting as deck hand recalls throwing out the whole main bow mooring rope in the hope of making fast on the landing stage bollard. Unfortunately, not only did he miss the bollard but he also failed to attach the other end to the ship. The inevitable result was that the rope slipped gracefully into the river, never to be seen again!

In 1956, further tonnage was prescribed for the Wallasey fleet and the order went to James Lamont & Co. at Port Glasgow on the Clyde. Unknown to the authorities at the time, she was to be the last of a long line of ferries built for Wallasey County Borough Council in its own right. Named **Royal Daffodil II**, she was delivered in 1958, had an additional deck and was generally far larger than the **Leasowe** and the **Egremont**. She had cost £282,160 to build compared with the £300,800 attributed to the **Royal Iris** back in 1951. Her overall length was 159 feet and with a beam of 49 feet and a tonnage of 609 tons gross, her payload of 1,950 passengers (maximum) was very substantial. The **Royal Daffodil II** carried the Wallasey Borough coat of arms on each side of her well proportioned, slightly rakish funnel. Sadly, later she lost this hallmark at the time of the merger of the two ferry fleets. Unusually, she had a small gaff rigged on her first wooden mainmast, but this was subsequently replaced with an all steel mast. The gaff was renewed several times but was no longer fitted when the masts became steel in 1976. She ran her trials on 14th April 1958, on the Skelmorlie mile and was delivered to the Mersey and handed over on 20th. She had a short break from her normal ferry and cruising work on 5th, 6th and 7th May 1964, when she sailed to Llandudno (normally the preserve of the little North Wales motorship, **St. Trillo** ex **St. Silio**, 1936/314 gross tons) to act as tender on 6th May for the Swedish cruise liner **Kungsholm**.

On the **Egremont** and the **Leasowe** (just like the **Royal Iris**) their original Lloyds classification also provided for sailings to Barrow, Holyhead and Caernarvon, but this was a facility they never used.

However, in 1970 the Ferries Superintendent at Wallasey did look into the feasibility of basing a ferry at North Wales to help fill the void left after the **St. Trillo** was permanently withdrawn by P.& A. Campbell Limited at the end of 1969 season. The intention was to run trips between Llandudno and Menai Bridge with cruises to Colwyn Bay, Red Wharf Bay and Puffin Island. Fares were fixed at 6/- (30p) for the Puffin Island cruise and 12/6d (62p) for a return ticket between Llandudno and Menai Bridge. It was agreed with the Board of Trade that they would grant the necessary Class III passenger certificate to enable 650 passengers to be carried on the **Egremont**. Seemingly, her only deficiencies were as follows: She would need a set of new lifejackets and somewhere to stow them; estimated cost £2,498. Alterations to crew accommodation would cost £1,500 and even then, the ship would have had to spend each night at Menai Bridge with the crew billeted ashore. In contrast, the crew of the **St. Trillo** had cabins aboard and slept on the ship. Lastly, the **Egremont** would need two lifeboats and for this purpose, it was intended that she would "borrow" the one from the **Leasowe** if the plan proceeded. Alternatively, the Board of Trade said that the **Royal Iris** (which still had her own two side slung lifeboats) could take up station at Menai Bridge without any additional work being necessary.

In the event, the calculations showed that over 50,000 passengers would have to be carried each season for the service to break even and the likelihood of this being achieved regularly was thought to be remote. Sadly, the plan did not come to fruition.

The **Royal Daffodil II** was a handsome vessel but, like the **Royal Iris**, with all her extra height and bulwarks forward, was difficult to handle. She would have benefited from more powerful engines than those with which she was fitted which were almost the same as those of the smaller **Leasowe** and the **Egremont** but with the addition of manually operated air brakes to assist engine movements. Nowadays, to build such a ferry without a bow thruster would be unthinkable. All the ferry captains use the forces of the tides to help them bring the ferries alongside safely but at slack water, especially with some beam wind in the wrong direction, for an underpowered ship like the **Royal Daffodil II**, berthing could be something of a trial.

In the spring of 1967, Wallasey Corporation approached General Steam Navigation Limited (G.S.N.) to see if they still required the use of the name **Royal Daffodil**. It should be remembered that G.S.N. had christened their magnificent Thames and cross-Channel excursion steamer **Royal Daffodil** (1939/2,061 gross tons) after the demise of the original 1906 built ferry their Medway associate had bought from Wallasey Corporation bearing the illustrious "Royal prefix".

The approach elicited the information that G.S.N. had taken their ship out of service for disposal. The name was duly relinquished and a year later, Wallasey Corporation were able to rename the **Royal Daffodil II** by dropping the "**II**" from the name.

Thick fog, for which the Mersey is renowned, had descended on the river on 5th January 1968, and the **Royal Daffodil** collided with a barge causing the ferry to be holed. After hastily disembarking her passengers and with her pumps working hard, the **Royal Daffodil** set sail for shallow water in the Guinea Gap (adjacent to Seacombe promenade) where classic pictures have been seen of her with her bows settled well down in the water and the vessel tied to a lamp post in order to discourage any further attempts at sinking! She returned to service on 23rd January having been relieved by the **Royal Iris**.

Merger of the Birkenhead and Wallasey ferry operations

Big changes followed the 1968 Transport Act under which, the Birkenhead and Wallasey ferries were stripped of their autonomy and both passed to a single authority known as the Merseyside Passenger Transport Authority. Later, in 1974, the Merseyside Metropolitan County Council evolved, thus changing the constitution of the Authority and its operating Executive.

In August 1974 the Woodside ferry was threatened with closure to take effect from 1976, but the ferry did not close. Twelve years later, Parliament abolished the Metropolitan County Councils and once again, the ferries found themselves under the aegis of a new authority comprising representatives from the five districts which Merseyside comprises.

"Merseytravel" became the composite trading name for the ferries, buses and local train network. An obvious manifestation for the Birkenhead and Wallasey ferry fleets, then newly combined under the one authority, was that they lost their separate funnel liveries. Gone were the distinctive black, red and black Birkenhead and black, white and black Wallasey colours and in their place, a uniform (and some traditionalists might say hideous) primrose yellow and pale blue version was applied. By May 1970, the **Mountwood**, the **Woodchurch** and the **Royal Daffodil** had the new livery, followed shortly after by the **Overchurch**, the **Leasowe** and the **Egremont**. The **Royal Iris** was excused the treatment, no doubt on account of the fact that her true funnels were actually square exhausts well aft of the obvious funnel which was a dummy and housed the ship's water tanks.

In 1974, the ferries' funnel livery became bright emerald green with a black top. In relative terms that was something of an improvement on the yellow, but was still quite shocking to lovers of the old, separate fleets. The **Royal Daffodil** suffered most as her once strikingly attractive funnel received only a thin black strip across its top. In any event, admirers could not readily understand why the ferries' funnels had to match the council controlled bus fleets!

The shape of things to come became much clearer when the Birkenhead ferry **Overchurch** was found operating to Seacombe for the first time on 31st January 1974, and frequently, thereafter.

In the name of economy, rationalisation and with the Woodside ferry under death sentence anyway, during the ensuing two years, the new joint service policy committee pronounced the **Leasowe**, the **Egremont** and eventually the larger **Royal Daffodil** as being surplus to requirements and available for sale.

The **Leasowe** was the first to go as a result of the merging of the operations and some alterations to the Seacombe landing stage which enabled the former Birkenhead ferries to call there. At a price reported to have been £34,000 she was sold in early 1974 for service in Greek waters. On 14th May 1974, (with all her openings boarded up) she left the Mersey renamed **Naias II** and registered in Panama. Almost completely rebuilt so as to be quite unidentifiable and, from 1980 bearing the name **Cavo Doro**, she was recently in the news having been taken out of the water and shown sitting high and dry at Morocco where she had been offered for sale. Lloyds Register of Shipping show ownership of the vessel as being the Overseas Atlantic Supply Corp., agent Carina Shipping of 15, Heyden Street, Athens, Greece.

The **Egremont** was withdrawn in 1975 and remained idle for a year. Whilst laid up in the Morpeth Dock, the vessel

*The **Leasowe** seen on 29th April 1970 in the traditional black and white colours of the County Borough of Wallasey which she was about to surrender for the yellow of M.P.T.A.* photo: Malcolm McRonald.

*The former Mersey ferry **Egremont** returning to "The Bag" at Salcombe after being towed to Falmouth for repainting in October 1989. The tug used for the main tow was unable to cross the sand bar marking the entrance to Salcombe therefore, the **Egremont** had to be nursed to and from her berth by local small craft.* photo: Richard Danielson.

sprang a leak causing serious flooding and damage to her electrical circuits and equipment to the extent that it was very unlikely that she could ever operate again without major repairs. In November that year she was sold to Frederick Oldham Limited of Liverpool in whose hands, her machinery was removed prior to the ship being sold on to the Island Cruising Club of Salcombe in Devon. She was towed from the Mersey on 15th June 1976. In Salcombe, in a beautiful sandy cove, the former Mersey ferry is still in use as a floating dinghy and sailing headquarters and has hardly changed in her appearance. Apart from having to be towed to Falmouth for bottom painting and maintenance, the ship has not moved.

In 1977 the **Royal Daffodil** was disposed of and, renamed **Ioulis Keas II** was sold for service in Greek waters. Now rebuilt so extensively so as to be virtually unrecognisable, the ship is still operating and is owned by Naftiki Eteria Kythnou, of Athens. This just left the **Royal Iris** as the sole remaining unit from the old Wallasey Corporation ferry fleet.

In 1977, a society called "Friends of the Ferries Across the Mersey" was incorporated to try to secure and promote the future operations and well being of the threatened ferries. They continue to thrive.

Thereafter, from time to time the future of the ferries came up for discussion at the highest level. In 1977, the Merseyside Passenger Transport Act was promoted in the Houses of Parliament and was described as "A Bill to authorise the discontinuance of ferry services etc..." The Bill failed. Threats of closure of the Birkenhead service became more and more common, the matter receiving formal mention again in a report by Merseyside's County Planning Officer towards the end of 1980. By then, it was reported that the ferries were losing £1,500,000 each year and that passenger traffic had fallen to a daily total of some 3,300 return trips (only about one tenth of the figure carried in the heady 1920s). This, the

lady planning officer compared with 58,000 using the road tunnels and 22,000 on the Merseyrail electric trains running under the river. Four other options were offered including abandoning both Birkenhead and Seacombe in favour of an entirely new Wirral based terminal. The farsighted (if not prophetic) report also suggested a triangular service the basis of which, a decade later, turned out to be the standard "shuttle" product.

However, in 1982 some experiments were carried out using a high speed twin hulled craft on charter from Western Ferries (Argyll) Limited. The **Highland Seabird** duly arrived at Liverpool on St. Valentines Day, 14th February 1982, having been sheltering in Douglas, Isle of Man for several days prior to her debut on the Mersey. For three days following her arrival, she was to be seen carrying out trials. Later, she returned to the Mersey again, this time in May and stayed about a month before taking up further charters on the Thames.

Clearly, the ferries' authority thought that the **Highland Seabird** had a long term future with them and at the end of the year she returned once more. However, on 20th December 1982, she was involved in a worrying incident. The craft had left the Liverpool stage with 90 passengers aboard bound for Woodside. Before she was properly underway, fierce winds and a strong tide combined to drive the **Highland Seabird** behind the landing stage where she became trapped and damaged. She and her passengers remained prisoners for almost an hour until the **Royal Iris** ventured to their rescue and managed to tow the unfortunate high speed craft to safety.

Despite a lot more talk about the possibility of small, fast passenger ferries like the **Highland Seabird** and also hovercraft, the decision was finally taken to rebuild the dilapidated Woodside landing stage and stay with the conventional ferries.

Shortly before her departure to Greek waters on 14th May 1974, the **Leasowe**, renamed **Naias II,** is seen boarded up for the long journey (which she accomplished under her own "steam") and carrying extra lifeboats.   photo: Ray Pugh.

Heavy silting of the berth at New Brighton was a major problem! photo: Ray Pugh.

The Wallasey Borough coat of arms was proudly carried on the stylish funnel of the **Royal Daffodil II** and the "Iris" had hers mounted forward on the main superstructure. Both were to lose this hallmark after the ferry fleets were merged following the Transport Act 1968.   photo: Malcolm McRonald.

*The **Woodchurch** pictured on 3rd January 1981, makes a fine sight as she crosses the mighty Mersey from Seacombe to Liverpool in choppy conditions. Running with a full flood tide, the author has "clocked" the ferries sailing at 18 knots!*
photo: Richard Danielson

The high speed catamaran **Highland Seabird** *had several evaluation trials on charter on the Mersey in 1982 but in the end, proved to be too small and was declared unsatisfactory. Finally, after more charters elsewhere, she was sold by her Scottish owners, Western Ferries (Argyll) Limited, for service in the Channel Islands. In the early 1970s both Birkenhead and Wallasey Corporations had looked at the feasibility of running a SRN 6 hovercraft on their respective ferry services. Similar experiments were again carried out 20 years later but the idea has not been commercially pursued.*

photo: John Shepherd.

To see the present picture in perspective, it is necessary to look back to 1957 at which time, as we saw earlier, Birkenhead Corporation had a fleet comprising four, quite delightful but old fashioned, coal fired steam ferries.

In the November of that year, Birkenhead Corporation contracted with Philip & Son Limited of Dartmouth, Devon to build two new ferries based on the design of the **Egremont** and the **Leasowe** which they had built for Wallasey Corporation, a few years earlier. Named after two local areas, the new ships were christened **Mountwood** and **Woodchurch**. They were launched into the beautiful River Dart on 6th July and 29th October 1959, respectively so that fitting out work on the **Mountwood** was well advanced by the time her sister, the **Woodchurch**, met her element. They were completed and handed over separately in 1960.

These two trim little craft were 152 feet long o.a. and had a beam of 40 feet. Their gross tonnages of 464 provided space on three decks for 1,200 passengers. On the upper promenade deck there was a forward shelter in which to sit, immediately beneath the bridge, as well as saloon accommodation both fore and aft on the main deck and a buffet/smoke room below. They were the first diesel powered ships in the Birkenhead fleet and Crossley Bros. Limited of Manchester constructed the two 8 cylinder engines which drove twin screws and developed almost 1,400 bhp. in total. The engines were fitted with special air brakes and a servo which Crossley's had developed for operation by the ship's captain when on the bridge, so that the main propulsion units could be stopped and reversed in rapid succession, thus aiding manoeuvring and safety.

18th March 1960 turned out to be a troublesome day for the then brand new Birkenhead ferry **Mountwood**. Gale force winds were lashing the Mersey as the **Mountwood** set off from Liverpool for Woodside. Her master, Capt. R. A. Flemming, reported that, on reaching the other side and being about to berth, both engines were at zero and he was allowing the **Mountwood** to set down onto the stage with the assistance of the tide and wind. He noted that the old coal fired ferry **Bidston** was also berthed on the Woodside landing stage, both vessels lying "floodway". On that day, the **Mountwood** was operating using traditional telegraph orders between the captain, engineers and the main engines, not direct bridge control. The records show that when the time came for "full astern" on the starboard engine to bring the ship to stop, in fact the duty engineer gave it "full ahead" by mistake. The result was inevitable!

With the following wind, and power from the errant engine movement, Capt. Flemming (using a masterly piece of restrained understatement) said "he was unable to prevent the **Mountwood** making contact with the stern of the **Bidston**". Capt. Flemming also noted in his report that as the ship's "wrong way" alarm (which should automatically give instant warning if an engine movement given does not accord with the telegraph instruction) was late sounding, he was denied any earlier opportunity to rectify the engineer's mistake.

In May 1961, the new **Mountwood** suffered a rare main engine failure whilst carrying a full load of commuter passengers across the river. In a textbook operation calling for very skilled seamanship, she anchored mid river and the **Woodchurch** came alongside her to take her passengers to safety.

In 1962, Birkenhead Corporation took delivery of a third, similar motorship which has proved to be the last vessel built for the service. The contract for this ship went to Cammell Laird & Company Limited on Merseyside, they having had a full order book at the time tenders were invited for the earlier pair. The new ship was named **Overchurch** and was the first Birkenhead ferry to be of "all-welded" construction. She was generally similar to the Dartmouth-built sisters although at

MERSEY FERRIES

(above) *The launch of the* **Woodchurch** *into the picturesque River Dart took place on 29th October 1959. photo: Richard Danielson collection.*

(right top and bottom) *Two views of the* **Mountwood's** *launching on 6th July 1959. Note the two propellers and twin rudders at the extreme quarters of the ship, positioned for maximum manoeuvrability. photos: Richard Danielson collection.*

The two "Royals" together! On 24th July 1990 the **Royal Iris** *well laden with passengers, cruises past the anchored liner* **Queen Elizabeth 2.** *The* **Woodchurch** *is alongside the liner acting as tender for passengers coming ashore.*

photo: Richard Danielson.

*The **Mountwood** sets off from Liverpool in gale force winds during a wild spell of weather in October 1991 and, as the ferry leaves, the Liverpool Pilot launch takes the opportunity of moving to a more sheltered position on the landing stage.*
photo: Richard Danielson.

the time, she alone had her wheelhouse spanning the whole breadth of the ship. The others each (originally) had a central wheelhouse and sidecabs. Her funnel, which is actually taller, appeared shorter than its counterpart on the **Mountwood** and the **Woodchurch** because there was a narrow bridge deck extension providing an alleyway abaft the funnel on the **Overchurch**. She was fractionally larger than the older sisters, being a few inches longer and having a gross tonnage of 468 tons. It was pleasing to note that these three new ships still carried on the tradition of having their names in script writing on their bows and at the time, they also acquired the slightly ragged looking, classic Birkenhead Corporation rope fenders to protect their rubbing strakes.

After the Birkenhead and Wallasey ferry fleets were merged in 1969, the ships initially remained on their respective native routes. From 1974 onwards, the lines of demarcation disappeared and thereafter, until the former Wallasey ferries were withdrawn, it was not unusual to see the ferries on either route.

As an economy measure, the **Woodchurch** was taken out of service in early 1981 and remained laid up in the Morpeth Dock for nearly three years. It was rumoured that she had been cannibalised to help keep the other two ferries running in the meantime. She was available for sale and was considered for purchase by various interested parties including one enterprising businessman (quite unconnected with the author) who planned to sail her on regular cruises around the Isle of Man! In the event, no sale materialised and during the late summer of 1983, the decision was taken to bring the **Woodchurch** back into service so that the frequency of a ferry leaving every 20 minutes could be restored.

1984 was the year Her Majesty Queen Elizabeth opened the International Garden Festival at Liverpool and it resulted in the ferries (mainly the **Overchurch**) operating a new service to Otterspool, adjacent to the festival site, commencing

on 3rd May. The **Royal Iris** spent the summer cruising normally and this left the **Mountwood** and the **Woodchurch** to run the two ferry services across the river. One particularly low tide in May saw the **Royal Iris** aground on a mud bank off Eastham with her passengers being entertained for two and a half hours until she refloated without further mishap. All the ferries received a cheerful new livery of red, white and blue in connection with the festival and later that year, were also very busy with the famous Tall ships, Parade of Sail.

Throughout 1985 there was also renewed optimistic talk of a new, smaller ship for the fleet, and for at least two of the ferries to obtain Class III passenger certificates to enable them to revive cruises out to the Bar Lightship and beyond. The following year, there was equal but opposite concern that the imminent demise of the Metropolitan County Councils (of which Merseyside was one) would put the ferries' whole future in jeopardy!

Talk of a barrage across the Mersey for power generation purposes brought discussion about new ferry tonnage and the revival of Liverpool Bay cruises, to an abrupt and indefinite halt. Two main positions for the barrage were considered as being possible, the first of which was on a line from Rock Ferry to Dingle, which would leave the ferries virtually unaffected. However, some proponents favoured constructing the barrage well downstream on a line running from Wallasey to Bootle. This would leave the existing ferry tracks upstream of the barrage, crossing water that would then almost always be smooth, thus enabling smaller, perhaps faster, more lightly constructed vessels to operate safely. At the time of writing. the project appears to be in abeyance.

During 1987, the whole matter of the ferries' future was churned up once again, and this time, the Merseyside Passenger Transport Executive decided to commission a feasibility report from consultants who were given a brief to include tourism and leisure as part of the ferries' long term aims. The selected consultants were L & R Leisure Plc. who had made a presentation of their case to members of the Executive and its Authority on 17th June 1987.

In the end, the results of these decisions were very far reaching and have given the final shape to today's modern Mersey ferry service.

Whilst these discussions were going on, the **Woodchurch** was unlucky enough to suffer a fire which put her lower deck buffet and shop out of action for a while. They were resited one deck higher until the damage was permanently repaired.

By July 1989, various parts of the long awaited Consultants' report were becoming public. Included in the report was the Business Plan containing the necessary tourism and leisure brief and it aimed to cut the annual deficit incurred by the ferries, which by then was running at £2,500,000. The report suggested that two ferries were to be upgraded as were the landing stages and terminals at a total cost of some £12,000,000, spread over four years but the other two ferries (one of which was the **Royal Iris**) were to be disposed of. In addition to the financial problems, there were difficulties in obtaining the agreement of staff to the necessary major changes to routine. In the event, the report was not adopted at the time and the consultants went "back to the drawing board" to revise their plans.

Eventually, new arrangements were agreed by all concerned and the initial sum of over £4,000,000 was set aside for various works. The **Woodchurch** was taken out of service for main engine repairs and refurbishment at the end of 1989 followed by the **Mountwood** shortly thereafter. Mannings Marine of Bootle, Merseyside won the contract. During the next six months or so, together the two ferries were transformed in what amounted to a major rebuilding of all the decks, passenger areas, catering and toilet facilities and their separate bridge wings and wheelhouses were all plated in (as on the **Overchurch**). In addition to work on the two ships themselves, the terminals and landing stages received substantial cash expenditure with fine new booking halls, retail shop outlets and other complementary services.

During this period, the **Overchurch** operated alone on a triangular service which proved to be the precise shape of things to come.

In order to execute the consultants' report, the Merseyside Passenger Transport Executive incorporated a new operating subsidiary company called Mersey Ferries Limited. On Sunday 1st April 1990, for an initial period of a year, L & R Leisure Plc., the consultants involved in the new master plan, took over the management of the ferries and the new service which was to start later in the summer.

Following in the wake of the Thames pleasure cruiser catastrophe and the loss of the **Marchioness**, with effect from 12th April 1990, all small passenger vessels had to implement effective new passenger counting systems to be able to determine accurately the number of passengers on board. To give effect to the new regulations, the Mersey ferries (which have always been very safety conscious) immediately brought in a system whereby passengers were counted on and off at each terminal and the resulting load noted on the bridge and conveyed orally to the landing stage duty officer.

The **Woodchurch** was the first of the rebuilt ferries to return to service which she did having been open to the public at the beginning of July. A few days later on Monday 16th July she was at Liverpool's newly rebuilt Ferry Centre for inspection by the press and local dignitaries who were invited aboard for breakfast. Universally, the results were pronounced as quite spectacular and without doubt, have resulted in the working lives of both the **Woodchurch** and the **Mountwood** being extended by many years.

*The **Woodchurch** giving her passengers a very rough ride in December 1966. For many people, the ferries were the only possible way to cross the river, whatever the weather!*

photo: Ray Pugh.

*The **Mountwood** leaving Liverpool landing stage in a storm on 28th October 1989.*

photo: Richard Danielson.

The next day, she commenced the new, triangular 50 minute cruise/ferry service and this became known as the "core product". It involves departing from Liverpool and sailing downstream on the Liverpool side of the river affording excellent views of the dockside and shipping. Off Egremont or thereabouts, the vessel heads across the river and back upstream to Seacombe where passengers are counted off and additional passengers come aboard. With everyone accounted for the ship sets sail again, still heading upstream for the short journey to Birkenhead where once again, some passengers depart the ship, new ones board, and others stay for the whole cruise.

Leaving Birkenhead, the vessel continues upstream passing Cammell Laird's Shipyard, and on up towards Tranmere and its famous oil refinery. Here the ferry crosses the river by turning to port once again and, keeping well clear of the Pluckington sandbank on the starboard side, heads back downstream for Liverpool and its well known Pier Head waterfront

In sympathy with the needs of regular commuters who travel to work by ferry, the service is amended during the morning and evening rush hour periods to make the crossings take as little time as possible. This is known as the "shuttle" and provides for a half-hourly service from the three terminals. Some regular users still march the decks whilst crossing the river to or from work, in an age-old tradition combining exercise, fresh air and a chance to meditate alone or to chat to fellow travellers. Such was the extent of the practice of walking the decks years ago, that the ferries all carried signs indicating the direction of flow for deck walkers!

It had been feared that the refurbishment of the *Mountwood* might not be ready for 24th July, the momentous date when the Cunard Flagship, *Queen Elizabeth 2* was due to visit the Mersey for the first time ever. However, the *Mountwood* certainly was ready and the entire fleet of four ships spent a wonderful day carrying over 20,000 passengers across the river and on cruises witnessing the event. In addition, two of the ships (*Overchurch* and *Woodchurch*) acted as tender for the liner's passengers once she was anchored in the river, just off the Birkenhead landing stage. The *Queen Elizabeth 2*, which was bound for the River Clyde on her round Britain celebratory cruise, left the Mersey on the evening of July 24th.

On 27th July, Prime Minister Margaret Thatcher travelled across the river on the *Mountwood* with Captain Dennis Titherington and other dignitaries.

After 24th July, the *Overchurch* was not much in demand and she took a well earned rest having provided, single handed, the temporary triangular service for the previous six months. By the end of 1990, some work had been carried out on the her and whilst she did not receive the major rebuilding work done on her near sisters, she then was dry-docked and well overhauled including being given a smart new coat of paint and new toilet facilities. The *Overchurch* is particularly well suited to river cruising and since the beginning of the 1991 summer has been engaged on weekend and other special theme cruising with family outings in mind.

On 12th April 1991, the *Mountwood* and the *Woodchurch* provided a late night cruise for the Merseyside Development Corporation. Each ship had 450 people aboard (the maximum they are permitted to carry on long cruises these days) and they sailed down river to off New Brighton to witness a firework display taking place at Fort Perch Rock marking the entrance to the Mersey. The event was to signal the start of the Merseyside Development Corporation's operations to completely rejuvenate New Brighton.

On 19th September 1991, the *Mountwood* was involved in an unfortunate accident when she ran out of control and crashed into the Liverpool landing stage causing considerable damage to her bows. She had to come off service forthwith and her place was taken by the ever-ready *Overchurch* which was slumbering in dock at Duke Street, Birkenhead.

"Thank you so much"! Prime Minister, the Right Honourable Mrs. Margaret Thatcher shakes hands with Capt. Dennis Titherington after her trip on the **Mountwood** *on 27th July 1990.*
photo: Capt. Dennis Titherington collection.

The **Mountwood***, beached on the sand at Egremont, awaits the tide to refloat her after brief attention to her rudders.* *photo: Ray Pugh.*

During their major refits, large portions of the decking of the **Woodchurch** *and the* **Mountwood** *were replaced.*
photo: Mersey Ferries.

*This tranquil scene shows the **Woodchurch** as she crosses the seemingly gentle River Mersey from Woodside to Liverpool. The oily smooth waters belie the fact than in just a few hours, they can be whipped up like a "boiling caldron" as shown on pages 62 and 63. Here, she is seen set against bright autumnal afternoon sun in 1984, with the cranes of Cammell Laird's shipyard, and Tranmere to be seen in the distance. In earlier times, this mile or so of riverbank was the site for ferry services to Woodside, Monks Ferry, (old) Birkenhead and Tranmere mentioned on page 11. photo: Richard Danielson.*

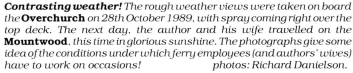

Contrasting weather! *The rough weather views were taken on board the* **Overchurch** *on 28th October 1989, with spray coming right over the top deck. The next day, the author and his wife travelled on the* **Mountwood***, this time in glorious sunshine. The photographs give some idea of the conditions under which ferry employees (and authors' wives) have to work on occasions!* *photos: Richard Danielson.*

The ferries sail in virtually all weather and being constructed to the highest possible standards, assure a safe if occasionally boisterous voyage for passengers. On 8th January 1958, a minor incident in which a passenger slipped over was reported. The following are the opening words. *"I am a captain in the employ of Birkenhead Corporation Ferries and have in fact 40 years service with the ferries, 9 as Captain. On Wednesday 8th January 1958, I was captain of the* **Thurstaston***. This steamer left Woodside at 13.10 for Liverpool. The weather had been stormy up to high water at 12.50 but after high water the weather moderated considerably. There was, however, a strong north-west wind blowing at the time but this was moderating. The* **Thurstaston** *arrived at Liverpool at 13.20. There was a slight swell in the Mersey but there was no difficulty in berthing or lowering gangways"* .... this shows the meticulous care taken to report all incidents in the records.

One day in the life of a Mersey ferry

In a typical day, either the **Mountwood** or the **Woodchurch** operates the service, with the other (together with the **Overchurch**) providing emergency relief sailings, summer season peak time back up and being available for private charters, special cruises and other bookings as required.

The crew of each ferry comprises six or seven men: a Captain holding the necessary river ferry Master's ticket, a Mate who holds a First Officer's river ticket, a Chief Engineer and a Second Engineer and two Seamen to deal with the gangways, ropes etc., and a lady catering assistant.

As day dawns, the first complete day crew join the service ship at Seacombe where she has been at rest overnight. If required, diesel fuel oil is taken on at Seacombe where a large tank, which is kept filled by road tanker, is provided for the purpose. During the night a part crew has been on board cleaning the ship thoroughly, attending to any work needed on the engines, bridge and other equipment and generally ensuring that all will be well for the next day's sailings.

After the two captains have conferred on the state of the ship, the weather, traffic in the river and any other vital matters, at 07.00 the first public voyage of the day takes place from Seacombe to Liverpool. Thereafter the ship runs a triangular "shuttle" service from Liverpool to Birkenhead and on to Seacombe, before returning direct to Liverpool. At 10.00 the route is extended into the "core product" elongated cruise described earlier in the text but sailing in the opposite direction round the triangle. At 14.00 the crew changes and once again, the outgoing captain appraises the relieving skipper of everything he needs to know about the day's events. In the late afternoon when the cruise business is over for the day, the ferry reverts to the short "shuttle" but remains running in the same direction as the cruise routine. As evening draws on and the ship shows her navigation lights to other craft in the busy river she keeps going on her triangular cross river ferry run.

In the course of a single, normal day's running, a daily total of over 120 arrivals and departures are written into the basic weekday timetable which is quite a test both for the ship, her engines stopping and starting and her hard working crews. The last ferry gets to Seacombe at 21.00 (earlier in winter) when the crew leaves the ship and the night crew join to tackle the day's cleaning and maintenance programme. Any major running difficulties or problems are reported to Captain Dennis Titherington who is the Ships' Manager or Marine Superintendent. A qualified river captain of many years' standing, Captain Titherington is normally based at Head Office at Seacombe and he deals with all aspects of the ships' planning, operations, routine dry-dockings, surveys and the occasional emergency that crops up.

The two ferries not on service remain in dock at Birkenhead where their own crews carry out a program of chipping, repainting, scrubbing and generally maintaining the fabric of the ship. Here too, the engineers can undertake larger maintenance jobs on the ferries' engines and machinery which, at the age of over 30 years, call for an ever growing engineering commitment.

Normally, either the **Mountwood** or the **Woodchurch** work the ferry service between them, alternating every two or three weeks.

> **Memo from the General Manager, Birkenhead Ferries, Woodside** to the Engineer in charge of the **Bidston** in January 1953. *"Your vessel, the **Bidston**, was blowing off steam this morning at the Woodside Stage both at 11.15 and 11.45. The Tides are only 23 feet and as it was just flood tide, there is no necessity for a high head of steam sufficient to raise the safety valves whilst your boat was at the stage. Please see that this does not happen again as it is a waste of fuel and water and does the boilers no good".*

1990
'FAREWELL TO THE ROYAL IRIS'
FINAL SEASON

RIVER MERSEY CRUISES

ON BOARD THE FAMOUS
ROYAL IRIS
RIVER MERSEY CRUISER
1951 – 1990

£4.00

MERSEY FERRIES

0300

AUGHTON F.C.

End of Summer Cruise
on the luxurious "Royal Iris"

ON SATURDAY 5th NOVEMBER 1983
Sailing from Liverpool Pierhead
Sailing 8.oop.m. Returning oo.3oa.m.

DISCO   Ticket £2.75

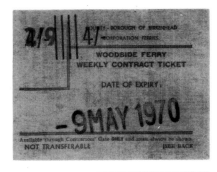

COUNTY BOROUGH OF BIRKENHEAD
CORPORATION FERRIES.
WOODSIDE FERRY
WEEKLY CONTRACT TICKET
DATE OF EXPIRY
- 9 MAY 1970
Available through Contractors' Gate ONLY and pass doors be shown
NOT TRANSFERABLE   SEE BACK

WALLASEY CORPN. PASSENGER TRANSPORT
ISSUED SUBJECT TO CORPORATION
BYE-LAWS AND REGULATIONS
DANCE CRUISE
WITH BAR AND BUFFET
ADULT 4/6
TICKET TO BE GIVEN UP AT
TICKET BARRIER ON RETURN

37882

Ticket No. **04501**

FESTIVAL GARDENS
FERRY SERVICE
19 85
PIERHEAD VIA WOODSIDE
TO OTTERSPOOL
ADULT

40p
SINGLE FARE

MERSEY Ferries

04-10-91 04-10-91 20:02

P IERHEAD X

S.A.R. ADULT
£ 1.50

COUNTY BOROUGH OF BIRKENHEAD
WOODSIDE FERRY
ONE PASSENGER   Fare
To or From LIVERPOOL   2½d
This Ticket must be given up at
the Contractors' Gate

3E 44454

Wallasey Corporation Ferries
N.D.L.B.
Dockers return from Duty
This Ticket of no value to be
given up at Barrier.

014148

No. H 2831
Mr.
Miss   (NOT TRANSFERABLE)

21 JAN 39

WALLASEY CORPORATION FERRIES
DANCE CRUISE
WITH BAR AND BUFFET
ADULT 3/-
Ticket to be given up at Steamer

D 04638

A selection of tickets from Wallasey and Birkenhead Corporation ferries,
including Rock Ferry and interesting cruise tickets from the period 1939 to 1991,
from the collections of Mac Fenton, Malcolm McRonald and Richard Danielson.

69

"Let the Lower Lights be Burning" — *immortal words of the famous mariners' hymn*

(above) *The* **Woodchurch** *seen at night in January 1991, gliding up the river to come alongside at Liverpool. The bright lights and ventilation tower at the other side of the Mersey are at Birkenhead.*
photo: Richard Danielson.

(top right) *The ferry terminal at Liverpool on the night of 6th October 1991 with the* **Mountwood** *making the last run of the day.*
photo: Richard Danielson.

(bottom right) *On board the* **Mountwood**, *on the last ferry run of the day from Birkenhead. Normally the ferry arrives at Liverpool and then sails a single trip to Seacombe where she lies overnight.*
photo: Richard Danielson.

An evocative night time study of the **Royal Daffodil II** *(1934).*

photo: Merseyside Record Office.

Merseytravel, the brand name of Merseyside Passenger Transport Executive (M.P.T.E.)
A statutory authority responsible for the operation of the Mersey Ferries following the abolition of Merseyside County Council.

Mersey Ferries Limited
(operating company owned by Merseytravel)

Mersey Ferries Limited Board of Directors
comprising: Chief Executive and Director General, Finance and Commercial Director, Passenger Services Director, Clerk and Support Services Director, Chairman of M.P.T.E., all of Merseytravel, the Chairman of L & R Leisure plc, and the General Manager of Mersey Ferries.

Management Team
and their respective seagoing and shore based staff comprising:
Support Services Manager together with his staff of two administrators, three inspectors, receptionist/typist, clerk/typist, storekeeper. **Marketing Executive** and her assistant. **Retail Manager** with two senior sales assistants and two sales assistants. **Technical Manager** with a senior maintenance chargehand, two maintenance chargehands, seven craftsmen and five semi skilled craftsmen. **Ship's Manager** with seagoing crews comprising: seven captains, six mates, six ship's engineers, six assistant engineers and twelve deck crew. **Catering Manager** with a catering supervisor (vessels) and two cook supervisors (terminals). **Terminals Manager** with a staff of nine chargehands, thirty nine seamen collectors and six seaman security personnel.

Some senior ferries' personnel

(top left) *Christine Melia, Marketing Executive.*

(top right) *Ian Thompson, General Manager.*

(bottom left) *Capt. Dennis Titherington, Ships' Manager (Marine Superintendent)*

the Royal Iris

VISITS THE RIVER
THAMES
3rd May to 14th May 1985

Welcome to the Royal Iris on
her first visit to the River Thames

Merseyside County Council

Nº 1750
Wednesday

Ticket £1
Admit One

25p TOWARDS COST OF MAIN MEAL
FOR ONE PERSON

Royal Iris
Dance Cruise

with Dining Facilities

This Ticket admits the bearer to Cruise Ship, use of facilities
and token (25p) towards cost of a main meal.

Sailing from Liverpool Pier Head 8 p.m.

*Archive material
from the collections
of
Mac Fenton
and
Richard Danielson.*

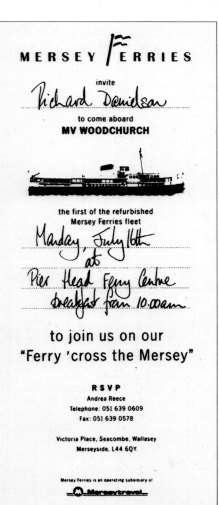

MERSEY FERRIES

invite

Richard Danielson

to come aboard

MV WOODCHURCH

the first of the refurbished
Mersey Ferries fleet

*Monday, July 16th
at
Pier Head Ferry Centre
breakfast from 10.00am*

to join us on our
"Ferry 'cross the Mersey"

R S V P
Andrea Reece
Telephone: 051 639 0609
Fax: 051 639 0578

Victoria Place, Seacombe, Wallasey
Merseyside. L44 6QY

Mersey Ferries is an operating subsidiary of

Merseytravel

The **Mountwood** at Seacombe in 1984. The bell looks as if it could do with some "elbow grease"! The legend on the banner aboard the ferry suggests that lobbying for the abolition of the six Metropolitan County Councils was already gathering pace (see page 50). In the distance to the right of the lifebuoy, we see the Royal Liver Building with its famous clock towers and liver birds (built 1911), the Cunard Building (1916) and the green copper domed Mersey Docks and Harbour Board Building (1907). St. Nicholas' Church, mentioned in the text on page 9, is obscured by the red lifebuoy. photo: Richard Danielson.

*24th July 1990 will long be remembered as the day that the **Queen Elizabeth 2** visited the Mersey for the very first time. The ferries were kept busy that day carrying 20,000 passengers as well as acting as tender for the liner.*   *photos: Richard Danielson.*

The future

It is a happy coincidence that publication of this book occurs early in 1992, a century and a half after the Mersey ferries began the process of coming under local government control.

The ferries have seen some radical changes to their operations and services recently and once again, it seems pleasantly realistic to think of ferries crossing the mighty River Mersey for many years to come.

The key to a lasting future lies with a continuing process of improvement to meet the evolving needs of the public at large. If the ferries were ever guilty of anything in the past, it was the old and familiar failure of local government concerns to recognise the rate paying public as their customers! Today, Mersey Ferries have grasped their opportunity and are well into the sometimes painful process of adapting to meet new challenges. In so doing they will make many friends and inevitably a few enemies.

Having improved the ships themselves and the three ferry terminals beyond all recognition, the ferries' management team are in discussions with the local authorities too. This will ensure an active involvement in projects aimed at rejuvenating the Liverpool Pier Head, Woodside and Seacombe areas.

The three ferries are beginning to age gracefully but most visitors both expect and enjoy the historic ambience created by their well scrubbed wooden decks, mahogany seats and polished brass. Eventually the ships will have to be replaced but with the continuing care and regular maintenance that is lavished upon them by their officers and crews, there is no reason why they should not have many years of life ahead of them.

As to the shape of the next century's Mersey ferry, who knows? High speed, surface skimming craft seem to be an alternative being considered by the world's major operators. On the other hand, it is hard to fault the logic shown forty years ago by Wallasey County Borough Council ferries' committee when they purchased the diminutive *Channel Belle* for economic late night ferry work and off peak cruising. Whilst she was clearly too small for many purposes, a ship of her dimensions might well suit a ferry route up-river of the proposed hydro-electric barrage, if and when it is ever built. The present incumbents owe their design to over a hundred years of improvements and enhancement and are still very efficient movers of large numbers of passengers.

It is not easy to make a direct comparison of passenger numbers carried these days, with those mentioned on page 34. The present figures are shrouded by concessionary travel, zone cards and the inaccuracy of apportioning numbers to cruise passengers. However, a yearly figure of approximately 1,000,000 is thought to be a fair estimate and this is expected to rise as the service continues to reap the benefits of further development.

At present, the withdrawal of the *Royal Iris* has left the fleet with no immediately suitable successor with which to fill the void. For as long as can be remembered, there has been a vessel for cruising, entertainment, recreation and functions. Hopefully, funds will be found to put into effect plans for the *Overchurch* to have a new dance floor fitted and top deck bars and provision for entertainment. Even better, but at greater cost, she could be upgraded to Class IV or III passenger ship standards and thus be able to make short excursions outside the Mersey.

Trips out into Liverpool Bay, to North Wales and along the Lancashire coast might once again become a reality. Remembering that it is not that long ago that people came from all over England's north west and North Wales to cruise the waters of the Mersey, given the right products, there must be potential to encourage some of those millions of people to return once more.

Perhaps we may even see two ferries renamed *Royal Iris* and *Royal Daffodil* in order to perpetuate those hard earned titles bestowed by the King of England back in 1918.

Some interesting extracts from the Wallasey Corporation Ferries Rules and Regulations, 1930.

"No servant shall be allowed to receive any gratuity from the public"

"The Master shall cause the decks and cabins to be washed and well dried each morning"

"If any person falls overboard, the Master must make every exertion to save life"

"Removal of ashes from the Steamers. On no account must ashes be thrown into the river"

"Keeping clear of heavy seas. The Masters are cautioned that in rough weather they must navigate to keep out of heavy seas... as passengers become alarmed by the rolling of the steamers and the shipping of heavy seas"

"Stagemen's Duties. In mist, fog or falling snow the Stage Bell must be sounded three quick strokes .... times (New Brighton three, Egremont two, Seacombe once) every minute."

"Fogs. On all vessels, the Masters will order the watertight bulkhead doors to be closed when running in fog and the Engineer in charge will see that all such doors are kept closed whilst the vessel is underweigh in fog."

"Fogs. If two passenger boats are running, one boat shall stay at the Seacombe stage until the steamer arriving from Liverpool is sighted. Masters in charge of steamers on the goods service shall only sail in company with and astern of the passenger steamer proceeding in the same direction."

"Getting out the small boat (lifeboat). On the order being given to get the (small) boat out the boat must be launched in 45 to 50 seconds."

Some interesting extracts from The Wallasey Ferries and Piers Byelaws, 1935.

"In the case of a vehicle drawn by a horse or other animal the person in charge shall for the purpose of retaining control remain by the head of the horse or other animal"

"A person shall not sound or play upon any instrument, or sing, dance, pray, preach read aloud or be in a state of intoxication or beg on board any boat".

"A person shall not spit on any of the boats or ferries' premises"

"It shall be lawful for the Master in charge of a boat, or any police officer on board thereof, to direct any passenger on board such boat to occupy any such part thereof as such Master or police officer shall think proper."

"A person shall not make or record any bet, or gamble or play any game of chance or hazard on the ferries' premises or boats. A passenger by any boat who remains on board at the end of the trip shall pay the return fare."

"A person shall not moor or anchor in the River Mersey a vessel of any description within seventy yards of any of the ferries' premises unless such vessel is in distress and then only until it can be safely moved."

Some interesting extracts from Wallasey Corporation Ferries, Tolls and Charges 1920.

"Overhanging Loads. The Goods Steamers are not allowed to sail with the gangway down without special permission from the Ferries Manager."

"Double tolls will be charged on all bicycles, handcarts etc. carried on the night boats between the hours of 00.30 and 04.30 inclusive."

Famous, faithful, friendly, ferries' festive fun!
Unashamedly alliterative description of the important part the ferries play in the lives of the people of Merseyside. Here we see "Captain Santa" delivering his Christmas 1991 message by means less traditional than the reindeer and sleigh.   Photo: Mersey Ferries.

A photograph for the real enthusiast! *The date is 14th May 1971. At one end of the country, the author was aboard the P.& A. Campbell Limited diesel-electric motorship* **Westward Ho** *(ex* **Vecta***) whilst she was acting as tender for the Swedish cruise liner* **Kungsholm***, anchored in Walton Roads, near Bristol during her 1971 round Britain Spring Adventure cruise. On the same day at Liverpool, on the left of the picture, Campbell's other excursion ship the* **Balmoral** *had arrived from the Bristol Channel and is seen alongside the Landing Stage making ready for her nostalgic Coastal Cruising Association charter trip to Llandudno and Menai Bridge. Two days earlier, the author photographed the* **Balmoral** *as she set off from the Bristol Channel on her journey to Merseyside. Later that week, she sailed to Llandudno again and on to the Isle of Man to meet the arrival of the* **Kungsholm***, later broken up at Garston, Merseyside in 1986. The ferry on the right is the* **Leasowe***, originally built for Wallasey Corporation in 1951.* *photo: Malcolm McRonald.*

79

Acknowledgements

I would like to place on record, the debt of gratitude I owe to the several people who have helped me to make this book a reality.

In particular I would like to mention my friends John Collins of Hoylake and Ray Pugh of Southport, who have provided a wealth of information, contemporaneous notes made over the years and many photographs. The friendship and mutual ferry interest which I share with these gentlemen goes back years and is something I value above all else.

Malcolm McRonald of Heswall delved deep into his photographic archives for me and examples of his excellent work appear throughout this book. His mother, Gwendoline, launched the **Woodchurch** back in 1959 whilst his father was Chairman of Birkenhead Municipal Transport Committee.

The staff and records of the Imperial War Museum, the Public Records Office, Liverpool Maritime Museum and Records Office, Lloyds Register of Shipping, the Williamson Art Gallery, the Central Library Birkenhead and Earlston Road Library Wallasey, The City of Dundee archives and The Merseyside Record Office were all immensely valuable for their contributions too.

A number of seagoing and shore based staff of Mersey Ferries took a personal interest in my endeavours and spent time and energy answering my many questions and searching through their own collections for illusive material. Of these, I would particularly mention Captain Dennis Titherington, Mac Fenton, Eugene Davies, and Ian Thompson who were all, not only helpful but enthusiastic.

Lastly, but by no means least, I have to thank Christine Melia, Mersey Ferries' marketing executive. Christine's professionalism and devotion to duty immediately encompassed my project in a keen and helpful way that I have not experienced before in my many years of marine journalism.

I sincerely hope that their employer recognises that these people are excellent ambassadors for their company.

Other ferry books available from the author

If you have enjoyed reading this book about the famous Mersey ferries, you may like to know that the author has published or written several more titles in the last decade. They can be bought individually (prices as below), or all five if ordered together are offered at the special total price of £15.00 including p & p.

The Isle of Man Steam Packet Volume 2, second edition. Fully illustrated history with mainly colour photographs and other archive material, this 64 page book covers the whole past Manx fleet since World War 2 until 1990. £4.70 including p & p.

The Isle of Man Steam Packet Volume 1. Fully illustrated with mainly colour photographs, this 28 page book covers the fleet as it was in 1988. £1.90 including p & p.

The Manxman Story. The fully illustrated history of the famous classic Steam Packet ship **Manxman**, the last traditional passenger steamer. 30 pages, black and white photographs. Colour cover. £1.30 including p & p.

The Very Best of British. Book 1. Ten of Britain's favourite ferries, excursion steamers and cross-channel boats. 64 pages, full ships' histories and anecdotes, many superb, colour and black and white photographs. Includes: **Lady of Mann** (1976), **Invicta** (1940), **Glen Sannox** (1957), **Free Enterprise I** (1962), **Shepperton Ferry** (1935), **Freshwater** (1959), **Scillonian** (1956), **Caledonia** (1934), **Ben-my-Chree** (1966), **Royal Iris** (1951) £5.70 including p & p.

The Very Best of British. Book 2. Second book in the popular series as above, covers eight more firm favourites. Includes: **Balmoral** (1949), **Caesarea** (1960), **Keppel** (1961), **King George V** (1926), **Lord of the Isles** (1989), **Lord Warden** (1952), **Mona's Isle** (1951), **Ryde** (1937). £5.70 including p & p.

Books dispatched promptly to any address. Private sales and trade enquiries welcome.

Please send your order together with a cheque or postal order (payable to Ferry Publications I.O.M.) to Richard Danielson, Ferry Publications I.O.M., P.O. Box 1, Laxey, ISLE OF MAN.